MW00826241

"Derek Ruth led a normal childhood until experiencing a critical brain injury on the football field at age twelve. His journey since the injury is a remarkable account of determination, effort, spiritual revelation, and support of family, friends, and the medical community. His story will inspire the reader to realize what the human spirit is capable of."

—TOM OSBORNE
University of Nebraska Cornhuskers Coach from 1973-1997
and College Football Hall of Fame Inductee

"I first met Derek Ruth in 2013, shortly after my appointment as the Catholic Bishop of Lincoln. Getting to know Derek as a friend, and hearing his remarkable story of faith, courage, trust, resilience, and acceptance, has profoundly moved me as a bishop. Derek's deep Catholic faith, nurtured by devout parents, continues to inform his life, providing him with a firm foundation for his hope, purpose, and motivation to move forward in life day after day. Through hard work, discipline, and perseverance, and with the heart of a true athlete, Derek continues to provide true hope for all of us, particularly as he describes in vivid language the long and enduring road of rehabilitation.

Everyone is created in the image and likeness of God and is given a mission and purpose in life. Our dignity and worth are not determined by what we do or produce in life, but by who we are as beloved sons and daughters of a good Father. Derek's story of survival, perseverance, hope, and determination after suffering a severe traumatic brain injury at the age of twelve is an inspiration for all. Derek went on to complete high school and graduate from college, and his story needs to be told.

Derek had an extraordinary encounter with Jesus, face to face, during his extended coma. He describes his encounter with Jesus in great detail. Derek's encounter with Jesus is both believable and convincing. He could have easily surrendered to the peace and tranquility of being eternally united to God in heaven with the Blessed Virgin Mary, the angels, and the saints, but instead, he knew that God had another purpose for his life on earth. He was given a mission to remain on earth and to lead others to encounter the living Lord in this world.

Throughout Derek's long road of rehabilitation, he experienced multiple supernatural encounters with Jesus, Mary, and the saints. He takes us with him on his pilgrimages to Lourdes, Rome, the Holy Land, and to the various shrines of our Catholic faith. Walking in the footsteps of Jesus and the saints, Derek's insights into the faith are remarkable. These encounters act as signposts along an epic journey into the meaning of life, faith, friendship, and future with hope as we all navigate our way through the trials and vicissitudes of life.

So much of life is just "showing up" and not giving up—moving forward each day with clear goals, hopes, and dreams. Derek demonstrates this in a remarkable way. With the support of a deep supernatural faith in God, along with the love and support of his family and friends, and the pastoral and sacramental accompaniment of numerous Catholic priests, Derek provides a roadmap for all of us. If we resist the temptation to "give up," we always win.

Derek's story also demonstrates that we are not alone in our life's journey. No man is an island. We need each other. We are not meant to walk through life alone. As Derek says, "it takes a team to get you through the tough times." Derek's life is a living testament to this profound truth. Reaching out to others in their time of need helps us to dispel the ugly lie of ungodly self-reliance that is so ingrained in our DNA as modern Americans.

May the story of Derek Ruth and his 'Eight-Minute Flight' be a source of inspiration for you and encourage you to live a future with hope."

—JAMES D. CONLEY
Bishop of Lincoln

"Working in college athletics for more than four decades, I have had an opportunity to meet many people who have inspiring stories, but few match those of Derek Ruth. I had an opportunity to watch Derek as a talented young athlete who fought for his life after a youth football injury. I personally got to know Derek as he pursued and achieved his goal of earning his degree from the University of Nebraska. His persistence, perseverance, determination, and positive attitude never wavered during a time when others in a similar situation would've felt sorry for themselves. Derek's story, as told in this book, will inspire you, give you hope, and help you understand that you should never give up, even if the odds you are facing seem insurmountable."

—DENNIS LEBLANC
Deputy Athletic Director for Student Services University of Nebraska

"I believe most of us, at one time or another, take ourselves and our abilities for granted. Watching Derek physiologically, physically, and psychologically learn and move, in spite of his imperception, inattention, neglect, agnosia, and neurologic alienation as a result of a traumatic brain injury has had a tremendous axiomatic impact on me. Anyone who worked with Derek and experienced his paradoxes witnessed scientific defiance through his organic, evolving human spirit and strength that made us all more mindful of the importance of being 'self-willed'. His dedication to himself, his belief in his family, his revelation in his faith, and his inquisitive self-nature resonate throughout this book of ongoing passion and persistence."

—RON HRUSKA, MPA, PT
Postural Restoration Institute, Founder

"Derek Ruth is an extraordinary individual whose strength and determination are truly inspiring. Despite a traumatic injury that ended his sports career, he has channeled his experiences into a powerful and moving book. His story is a testament to resilience and hope, and I am honored to support his remarkable journey."

—JAKSON REETZ
MLB player

THE
EIGHT-MINUTE
FLIGHT

*The Miraculous Story of the Boy who Chose
Earth Instead of Heaven*

DEREK RUTH

Scriptures marked RSV are taken from the REVISED STANDARD VERSION (RSV): Scripture taken from the REVISED STANDARD VERSION, Grand Rapids: Zondervan, 1971.

Fedd Books
P.O. Box 341973
Austin, TX 78734
www.thefeddagency.com

Published in association with The Fedd Agency, Inc., a literary agency.

Cover Design: Christian Rafetto (www.humblebooksmedia.com)
Insert photo of football field by Thomas Park on Unsplash

ISBN: 978-1-964508-10-8
LCCN: 2024909622

Printed in the United States of America

TABLE OF CONTENTS

FOREWORD

A young mother rose to greet me from the bedside of her twelve-year-old son, Derek, as I walked into the hospital room in Lincoln, Nebraska. *This is my worst-case scenario*, I thought, heart sinking. I saw myself in the woman. I felt her pain and hope, recognized the love, grief, and desperation in her eyes. I could feel the powerful prayers and faith that hovered over the room. I saw the way she looked at Derek and then me, as if I had some special answers or even powers to rewind the tape and erase what happened.

Derek Ruth was playing youth football on September 6, 2008, in Malcolm, Nebraska, on an ordinary blue-sky day. He was a talented athlete who played multiple sports and clearly had a bright future. With one play—just a twist of fate—he received a traumatic brain injury. In that instant, the trajectory of Derek's life changed. During the critical golden hour after a brain injury, Derek's medical team did everything right. Each minute counts after injury and as the brain swells, time is essential to save brain function and prevent death.

As I moved closer to the bedside and introduced myself to the Ruths, I glanced at Derek's head, as I had become accustomed to doing on traumatic brain injury ward visits. It was concave and sunken on both sides where the doctors had removed two separate parts of his skull bone to let his brain swell. The bone flaps were stored in his stomach cavity until he would be ready for his cranioplasty surgery. A white plastic helmet sat on the bedside table next to him. It was all too familiar.

I was touring the brain injury ward at Madonna Rehabilitation Hospital (one of only eight in America in its class) after delivering a speech to caregivers and families. The opportunity to meet families and survivors, though difficult, was an experience I cherished in the aftermath of our own hellish journey. It felt like paying it forward to be able to connect and meet others, like the Ruth family, who were traveling along the same road as our family. When my own husband was at Derek's stage of recovery, I remember wishing I could meet and talk to someone who had experienced what we were going through. While I lacked a crystal ball to see the future, it gave me a sense of purpose to listen to people's stories, answer questions, and share our journey.

The hospital setting, the brain injury ward, and the exhausted but hopeful expressions I saw around me had once been my day-to-day existence. While we were a few years ahead of the Ruth family, everything about the scene took me back in an instant.

On January 29, 2006, I was in Disney World with my four children when I got a phone call from the president of ABC News. My husband, Bob Woodruff, had recently been named the co-anchor of ABC's *World News Tonight*. He was in Iraq reporting on President George W. Bush's State of the Union address. This was supposed to be a very quick trip; get in and get out. He had been there nine times before, covering the war and embedded with the marines during the 2003 invasion—far more terrifying and lengthy situations. So, the phone call I received from Bob's boss, David Westin, came as a complete gut punch.

"Bob has been critically injured and has taken shrapnel to the brain," David said when I picked up the phone. "He's going into surgery now and you need to reach out to family before the news breaks." I began to crumble, to fall back against the hotel bed, and then, suddenly, I remembered there were four children sleeping in the next room. I had to keep it together, to be the strong one for all of us, including my husband. We had to get on a plane and make it home from Orlando. I needed to take this step-by-step, minute-by-minute, as the future without the love of my life was incomprehensible to me. *Baby steps,* I thought. *Don't try to imagine too far into the future.* What I saw when I met Bob was terrifying.

Bob had been traveling with the army, reporting about the progress our combined forces had made in cleaning up what had once been a very dangerous insurgent area in Iraq. Standing up in the top of the tank, rolling along a dusty road, a controlled improvised explosive device (IED) that had been buried hastily in the road was detonated about twenty-five yards away. Both Bob and his cameraman, Doug, were hit by the force of the blast and shrapnel. Luckily, Doug's injuries were more minor.

Rocks and shrapnel flew into Bob's face and back; some shattered his scapula under his flak jacket. One rock, the size of a quarter, cut through the chin strap of his helmet, which flew off, landing twenty-five yards away. That rock continued to travel across his neck, embedding just one-tenth of a millimeter from his carotid artery on the left side. The force of the bomb blast crushed Bob's skull, driving shards of bone into his brain and knocking him unconscious. Thanks to the amazing work of the military, the medics, and an incredible team of doctors and nurses in Balad and Baghdad, Bob's skull was removed within forty minutes from impact to relieve pressure and allow his brain to swell.

Bob would remain in a medically induced coma for the next thirty-six days, moving from Baghdad to the military hospital in Landstuhl, Germany, and then put on a plane within seventy-two hours to Bethesda Naval Hospital in Washington, DC, where our nation's injured troops receive the best care in the world.

At that time, unbeknownst to most of America, thousands of young men and women were coming home suffering both the visible and invisible wounds of war. The American public would soon learn more about these signature injuries of the war, but at the time of Bob's injury, the three letters "TBI" (traumatic brain injury) meant nothing to me.

The wars in Iraq and Afghanistan, America's longest-running wars, would teach us much about the psychological and neurological effects of trauma and damage to the brain. Those advancements would trickle down to help others, civilians like Derek who would receive excellent care that would give him the best chance at recovery.

Standing in Derek's hospital room, my mind reeled back to those days. Derek's beautiful, smiling face and slightly dull eyes were all too familiar. His youth and optimism seared my heart.

There is one worse thing than having this happen to Bob, I remember thinking when I walked into his hospital room in Germany and saw him, alabaster white, due to the frigid temperature in his room to keep down the swelling. *The worst thing would be if this had happened to our child.*

Bob had recovered extremely well, defying so many odds. And while we were still very much on our journey, I knew what lay ahead for the Ruth family. It was two steps forward and one back. And it wasn't just Bob who had been hit by the bomb— it was all of us. The injury and its effects would ripple out to touch every family member in varying ways. There would be so many times I would have to choose between being with Bob and being a present mother. As Jennifer Ruth would, I had to make peace with doing the best I could at the time, knowing I was missing so many things with my children.

While I knew Derek's age and neuroplasticity put the recovery odds in his favor, the frustrating thing about a TBI is that no one can (or will) give you a percentage of recovery or try to predict the future. Each brain is as individual as we are. I think of it as the last truly mysterious organ in our bodies. Although there is so much hope for what we can and will learn about neurodegenerative diseases and neuroplasty, there is so much more work to be done.

As I chatted with Derek, a gorgeous, engaged boy who should have been at school, I was reminded of the preciousness of life, of all the things we can take for granted if we don't stop and feel our gratitude. One minute, life can be golden, and the next, tragedy strikes on a clear day when you're running the ball down a football field.

The book you are about to read, *The Eight-Minute Flight*, is a book of courage, faith, family, recovery, determination, and grit. Over the years since meeting the Ruths, I have cheered from the sidelines as Derek has hit various milestones and watched in admiration as the family and community have surrounded him with love, encouragement, and the tools he needed to put one foot in front of the other. If only every TBI survivor had a support network like that!

Derek writes honestly of his depression and of coming to terms with a life he had not imagined and certainly had not planned for. His powerful description of seeing Heaven and meeting Jesus is a testament to the power of faith to keep us all going, something I felt in our own journey. I know you will enjoy this memoir because overcoming the hard things in life is simply part of the human experience, no matter who we are. And the people who have overcome the hard things, like Derek, are always the ones who have something to teach each one of us.

—LEE WOODRUFF

CHAPTER ONE

Regular. Usual. Nothing out of the ordinary. It was a warm, Indian Summer day and the Nebraska sky was extra clear and blue. Just another fall Saturday, and for my family and me, that meant football.

As was typical for us, the weekend schedule was full. Football all day Saturday, the wedding of a family friend Saturday night, and church on Sunday. Friday night, Mom made my favorite meal of hamburger gravy, mashed potatoes, and corn. She got up early Saturday morning to make a crockpot meal that would be ready by dinner time. Then we headed to the football field. My dad was a coach for my brothers and me. Mom helped run the concession stand. My brothers played in the morning. By the time my game kicked off in the afternoon, Dad was on the sideline with Mom and my brothers in the metal bleachers.

In the middle of the second half, I lined up at running back, got the ball on a sweep, and ran the football. As soon as I was hit from behind, I fumbled the ball. My mom saw my right arm drop oddly, almost in slow motion.

"There's groups of coaches everywhere, so we're all kind of flying around, and stuff is happening," remembers Michael Karel, a physician assistant who also was a coach. "Derek… it was weird. He fumbled the ball, which he doesn't do. I mean, he was never known to fumble the ball. Something was going on."

A teammate recovered the ball, so I got up and headed to the huddle, but the coaches called time out and sent me to the sideline. They could tell something was wrong. Coach Karel sat me on the bench and looked me in the eyes.

"What's going on, Derek? Are you hurt? Did you get hit in the head?"

"Nah, I didn't get hit, but my hair hurts."

Then Coach started asking me questions.

"What's today's date?"

"September 6, 2008," I answered.

"What's the score of the game?"

"14-0."

"Can you tell me your brothers' names?"

"Corbin. Connor. Trevor. Brenden."

Every answer was correct. He asked me again if my head or neck hurt. The only thing that hurt at that time was my hair. Minutes later, they told me I stood up and screamed, "My head!" pulled off my helmet and collapsed into Coach Karel's arms.

I didn't register the hush that settled over the field or hear the life flight helicopter coming from the horizon and landing on the fifty-yard line. Coach Karel remembers that the crowd was pushed over to the side of the field along with other players. An ambulance arrived first, and paramedics worked to establish an airway. As soon as StarCare landed, they transported me from the ambulance onto the helicopter to get to the trauma center as quickly as possible. One of the flight nurses knew they had to get me to the trauma center quickly. Time was not on our side. It was only an eight-minute flight, but every second was critical.

They lifted off and updated the hospital that they had a Level 1 trauma. I was intubated, which meant I had a tube down in my throat to help me breathe. And I was unresponsive. I was showing signs of posturing, which can be a sign of decreased oxygen to the brain, and there was also concern about increased cranial pressures, which can lead to brainstem herniation.

★ ★ ★ ★ ★

Before September 6, 2008, I was a pretty ordinary twelve-year-old kid, busy with sports, school, and being a big brother—but mostly sports. I wasn't just a kid who played sports; my life and my family pretty much revolved around sports. It was in my blood. My mom and dad played softball and football at the University of Nebraska at Kearney, and two of my uncles played football for the University of Nebraska Cornhuskers in the 1990s when they were one of the best teams in the country. I'm unbelievably competitive. That's something I get from my mom's side. Some of my favorite times were spent playing football and baseball in the backyard with my brothers.

I was really starting to get serious about sports. My years were divided into football, basketball, and baseball seasons. In January 2008, I resumed speed and acceleration training, something I really liked. I'd taken the fall off from training to give my body a break while I was playing football. I also decided to skip basketball that winter. I had been asked to play on the Lincoln Blaze select basketball team I'd been on the previous two years, but I wanted to focus on getting myself faster and more agile.

During my twice-a-week, one-hour workouts at Madonna ProActive in Lincoln, Nebraska, my trainers, Chris Range and Steve Tangen, pushed me to the max. They had me doing intense stuff like treadmill work and plyometrics. Treadmill work consisted of march walks with the treadmill at an incline, running at sixty to seventy percent of my full speed for a minute, then running full speed for eight to ten seconds. With the plyometrics, I did box jumps, single-leg box jumps, lateral jumping over foam blocks, and square jumps clockwise, counterclockwise, and diagonally.

When February came around, I began baseball practice at an indoor facility. I'd been part of the Lincoln Sox select team for the past three seasons. Indoor practice meant conditioning, stretching, fundamental work, hitting drills, and a lot of long toss to increase arm strength. Practice lasted two hours, so we spent forty minutes at each station. My favorite forty minutes was at the hitting station, where we did soft toss, hitting the ball off the bounce, batting with one hand to increase power and focus, tee work, and then hitting in the batting cages.

By the middle of March, the weather was decent enough that we could practice baseball outdoors. The season started in April. During our first couple of games, the weather was more like winter than spring, which made it tough to play because my hands would get cold. It warmed up before our first tournament in mid-April.

In May, I finished sixth grade. In the Fall, I'd be off to junior high at Malcolm Public Schools. The school was small and had just one building for kindergarten through twelfth grade. Weightlifting at the high school began as soon as school got out for the year, and I was able to start lifting in conjunction with my workouts at Madonna ProActive with Steve and Chris. That summer, when I was not working out or playing baseball, I usually hung out with my brothers. We played video games, went swimming in the pool behind our house, and played sports in the backyard. We got to see a couple of the College World Series games at Rosenblatt Stadium in Omaha.

In July, our Lincoln Sox baseball team went to a national tournament in Colorado. We won all three games in pool play relatively easily and were seeded in the top four for a double-elimination tournament. After we won our first tournament game on Thursday, my teammates and I went up into the mountains just to hang out and be together. Friday, we played two games, beating a team from Millard, Nebraska, and then losing to a team from Iowa. That night, we went putt-putt golfing and go-kart riding just to have fun.

On Saturday, July 12, we played our final game of the tournament. It came down to the last out, and we got beat by a team from Colorado on a walk-off single. The Lincoln Sox ended up placing fourth in the national tournament, and I had one of the most memorable weeks of my life.

In the latter part of July, I had a regular physical. I was perfectly healthy and cleared to play sports. Then, it was time for football. I was playing on two teams: my school's junior high team and a youth league team. Just four games were scheduled for our junior high team. The league had eight games against better competition. Practice began in the middle of August when school started. We practiced Monday through Thursday for the junior high team. Those practices were brutal because they were right after school.

Our first league game was Sunday, August 24. On offense, I played running back and on defense I played middle linebacker. We lost our first game. We didn't have a football game the following weekend because of Labor Day. Our next game was against Omaha Gross on Saturday, September 6.

★ ★ ★ ★ ★

After I collapsed, Coach Karel and others worked to get me stabilized while the call went to 911.

"He was not responding to my voice or any kind of stimuli," Coach Karel said. "That's when we knew we needed to move fast. We got his jersey and shoulder pads cut off. I can still remember Royce's (Derek's dad) hand, grabbing me on the back of the shoulder and asking, 'Is he going to die?'"

Paramedics from Malcolm Fire and Rescue and Lincoln Fire and Rescue arrived within minutes. The paramedics worked to open an airway, start an IV, and prep me for the flight. They assessed me and knew I had to get to a trauma center as fast as possible. They called in StarCare for a life flight to the Bryan Trauma Center in Lincoln. I learned this information by watching a documentary the hospital made two years after my injury.

Before the paramedics arrived, Coach Karel noticed I was posturing. My wrists crimped up, and my hands kind of turned inward. It meant oxygen wasn't getting to my brain. It's a bad sign of a head injury.

In emergency care, they talk about the 'golden hour.' To achieve the best outcomes, they want to get the patient to the hospital for immediate intervention within sixty minutes of sustaining an injury. StarCare landed on the helipad at the trauma center eight minutes after leaving the football field, and they transferred me to the hospital. From my collapse to my arrival, we were right at that golden hour. It was a miracle.

"It's unheard of," Coach Karel said. "From the time Derek went down on the field, we had him into the hospital and into CT and then straight to surgery. The indications I got when I talked to the neurosurgeons later was that within five more minutes, he wouldn't have made it."

Surgeons discovered I had an epidural hematoma (a brain bleed) on the left side of my brain. They performed a craniectomy in which they removed a piece of bone from my left skull to relieve cerebral edema (swelling). The bone flap was stored in the subcutaneous tissue in a pocket in my abdominal wall for preservation so it could be replaced later.

To decrease cerebral edema and protect my brain, I underwent therapeutic hypothermia. My entire body was cooled by liquids and medications. The trauma doctor initiated the protocol that involved cooling my body down to 32 degrees Celsius, as they had been seeing good outcomes with patients with head injuries like mine.

The process involved packing me in ice around my head, my neck, my groin, my armpits—all over my body. They also gave me IV saline that was cooled down and put iced saline down my gastric tube, which went into my stomach to cool it down. They discussed my case with the University of Pittsburgh and considered doing this when they got the trauma call that I was on my way in. I fit the perfect criteria with my symptoms, and the treatment would give me the best chance to retain brain function.

The idea was that they would be cooling down my brain cells as quickly as possible, which would decrease my metabolism and decrease the need for oxygen so I wouldn't have as much swelling. I was also placed upright on a tilt table. I was the first pediatric patient at the Bryan Trauma Center to undergo this treatment for a head injury.

But I was unaware of any of this because I was in Heaven, face-to-face with Jesus.

CHAPTER TWO

While I was in the helicopter, my dad, Coach Karel, and another coach got in a pickup with a state patrol officer and made the fifteen-mile drive to the trauma center at a high rate of speed. As they walked through the hospital doors, Coach Karel saw a nurse he knew.

"She just looked at me with tears in her eyes and shook her head," he said. "…I didn't even know if Derek was going to make it through surgery."

Mom arrived a short time later. When she heard the reports and the updates, she collapsed to the floor.

News of my injury spread quickly. A phone rang in a movie theater in Kearney, Nebraska, alerting one of my mom's college friends. Richard Baier, a close family friend, told our parish priest, Father Sean Kilcawley. Holly Schifsky, who would later become my inpatient occupational therapist, remembers hearing that a young man had been injured in a football game as she played with her boys in their backyard in Lincoln. At Memorial Stadium in Lincoln, my grandparents had just watched my uncles and the rest of the Cornhuskers defeat San Jose State 35-12 when they were notified that I had been badly hurt. Ron Hruska, who grew up near my grandparents in Ulysses, Nebraska, remembers the news shaking the community.

Extended family and members of our parish, sports teams, and community gathered at the hospital. The nurses and doctors told my parents I was in critical condition and prepared them for the worst.

During the three or four hours I was in surgery (none of us remember exactly how long that first operation lasted as time had lost all context), many of the fifty-some people in the hospital waiting room prayed. Four or five priests were there to support my family.

But I had left the hospital. I was with Jesus in Heaven.

I had no sense of leaving my physical body. When I was standing in front of Jesus, I could feel all my extremities. It was like I still had my earthly body, but everything was purified and glorified. The quality of the air in Heaven made my body feel amazing, especially my hands and feet. I cannot even describe how my skin felt. I was unaware of being either hot or cold. I just felt perfect. Whole and pure. Words cannot even come close to explaining the sense of peace, calmness, and encompassing love surrounding me.

But my focus was not on my own body or what was happening to me; my eyes were on Jesus.

The only way I can describe it is to say that the physical presence of Jesus is awesome! I have always been keenly aware of the physical appearance of others because of my time working out and because my grandpa, mom, and other family members are physical therapists.

Jesus was thirty-three years old, stood about five-eight, and weighed one-hundred seventy pounds. Jesus' arms were muscular, but the trap muscles in his neck were not defined. His feet were not terribly big; I would say about average size, but his calf muscles were muscular and defined. Jesus had holes in the middle of his feet. He had a beard and shoulder-length hair. His face was perfect and did not have any blemishes. It had a beautiful glow that was completely white—the whitest white I have ever seen.

And his heart! The heart of Jesus was just bursting with unconditional light. His hands were white, and his wrists had holes in them where the nails had gone through his flesh when he was crucified. I did not see the spot where the lance was thrust into his side. That was covered by the white robe Jesus was wearing.

Heaven is the most beautiful place ever. No sky or ground, just a never-ending expanse of white. I was standing erect, but nothing was physically holding me up. I had the sense of being held by the Holiness of Heaven. I strongly believe I could have flown in heaven, although I didn't try.

I have no real sense of how long I was with Jesus during that initial encounter. The next thing I remember being aware of was intense physical pain a few days after the surgery. Heaven is a lot different from Earth. In Heaven, things are relaxed, which means no physical stress or anxiety. Heaven is forever and is the same every day. There is no need for a calendar or a watch because what is there to be worried about in Heaven? The answer is nothing because everything you could possibly want is at your fingertips.

Faith has always been a big part of my life. I was baptized just a few weeks after I was born in 1995 and attended mass regularly with my family. I had my first confession and first communion in 2004. After I was confirmed in 2007 at the age of eleven, I began to pray the most Holy Rosary daily. The rosary is a religious exercise in which prayers are recited and counted on a string of beads or a knotted cord. A traditional Roman Catholic Rosary consists of 59 beads. The 6 large beads are used for praying the Our Father prayer, and 53 smaller beads are used for praying the Hail Mary prayer. I have always found great comfort and peace when I am saying the Rosary. It comes with many promises for those who faithfully pray it, and I have obtained everything I have asked for through it. The eighth promise of the Rosary states that at the moment of death, those who participate in the Rosary shall participate in the merits of saints in paradise. I believe that promise. To this day, I still have a devotion to the most Holy Rosary, and I have experienced ten other divine appearances since that first one in the hospital.

I was unaware of what was happening in the operating room but felt a point of decision. I could choose to remain living in paradise with Jesus or return to my life on Earth. It was a very tough decision. I think about it often. I chose to come back to Earth for the people who needed me and for the people I love.

While I was experiencing divine peace in Heaven with Jesus, my family was receiving regular updates from nurses. When the surgery was finally over, and I was in the ICU, the doctors told my parents I had survived, but we had a long road ahead.

"Initially, after the surgery, Derek was unresponsive," my mom told the documentary film crew. "They had started the cooling technique, and he remained cool for about thirty-six hours, and then slowly, they started to rewarm his body temperature. At that point, he did respond a little bit, a little bit of eye-opening, a little bit of hand movement."

My brain continued to swell, so I was taken back to the OR three days later, where I underwent a right-side craniectomy with another bone flap from my skull again banked in the subcutaneous tissues of my abdominal wall. My doctors were initially discouraged by my progress. After the first surgery, the radiologist saw a lot of cell death on the MRI. They were afraid I'd lose my sight. I had survived, which was a miracle, but the cell damage looked extensive.

The second night in the hospital, my good friend Maddie organized a prayer vigil. Growing up, we always had a tight relationship, like brother and sister. Maddie used to babysit me when I was young. So, when Maddie heard that I'd been badly hurt in a football game and was not expected to survive, she took action.

On Sunday, the day after my injury, Maddie's younger brother had a midget football game in Lincoln. Maddie was sitting with her mom in the stands and remembers thinking, "We've got to do something for Derek." She had the idea of getting some people together at the hospital to pray the Rosary for me. She began making calls while her mom started emailing people. Maddie called North American Martyrs, the parish my family attends, and asked them to start an email chain inviting people to meet at the hospital to pray.

Maddie clearly remembers showing up at the hospital thinking she would have maybe ten or fifteen people joining her, but hundreds of my friends packed the room. Maddie was in utter amazement.

"I just remember kneeling and praying the Rosary with Derek's friends, asking that Derek would survive and that a miracle would take place," Maddie said.

Her prayers were answered.

Two days after the second surgery, they did another MRI and doctors couldn't believe the results. Areas of my brain they thought dead were now showing signs of life. The radiologist couldn't believe that the images were from the same patient. The therapeutic hypothermia and the prayers of Maddie and my friends had worked.

CHAPTER
THREE

I don't remember much about my seventeen days in the ICU or the surgeries that led to saving my life. I don't remember the ambulance ride that took me three miles across town to one of the premier rehabilitation centers for traumatic brain injuries. I wasn't even aware I was about to become another first.

As I stabilized, my family faced big decisions. The hospital had saved my life, but what kind of life would it be? The prognosis wasn't great. They thought I would never walk or be able to live independently. As one of my occupational therapists described it, I was a two-month-old in a twelve-year-old's body. I needed intensive inpatient rehabilitation to begin retraining my brain and my body. My mom researched several facilities, but in 2008, not many places in the country offered pediatric rehab for my type of injury, and my family was definite about finding a place where rehabilitation was the number one goal. They had been told to buy a power wheelchair because I would never walk again. They said no. They said we were going to fight to regain every bit of ability possible. My mom and dad wanted the best rehab for me but also wanted our family to stay together. They had four other boys, including an eleven-month-old, to consider.

Madonna Rehabilitation Hospital sits in the middle of one of Lincoln's residential neighborhoods. It was started in 1958 by the Benedictine Sisters, who chose the name Madonna to honor the Blessed Mother. I wonder if they had any idea that fifty years later, a kid who wanted to stay on Earth to be with his family would need their hospital on that tree-lined street. In 2008, Madonna was one of only eight hospitals in the nation with Commission on Accreditation of Rehabilitation Facilities (CARF) accreditation for both inpatient brain injury and pediatric rehabilitation programs. But there was a problem. I was still using a trach to help me breathe, and at the time, Madonna had never admitted a pediatric patient with a tracheotomy.

Divine intervention comes in different forms. For my family at that moment, it came in the form of a dignified man who was and still is one of the most famous people in our state. Tom Osborne is a college football coaching legend who led the University of Nebraska's Husker football team to national championships in 1994, 1995, and 1997. Two of my uncles, Jeff and Joel Makovicka (my mom is their older sister), played on Coach Osborne's championship teams. Coach Osborne retired from coaching in 1998 but returned to the university as athletic director from 2007-2013. He was in that role when he heard about my collapse on the football field.

"I was very concerned when I heard about Derek's injury because I've been involved in football a long time and haven't seen very many like that. It was maybe a little bit touch-and-go for a while," Osborne said during a recent phone call. "I would have done anything I could for him. Of course, part of it's my connection to Joel and Jeff and their family, but more than that, even if we hadn't had that connection and I heard about somebody hurt on a football field like that, I'd have done the same thing."

What Osborne did was talk to the people at Madonna. Years of being involved in football meant he had close connections to the rehab hospital. "I was really concerned about Derek and prayed for him every day. You worry if we'll get him in there in a very short time because sometimes those places are really filled up."

Osborne's calls and his prayers, along with the hundreds of calls and prayers from other people, helped open the door for me to be the first pediatric patient to be admitted to Madonna while still on a trach. I was also the youngest patient they'd had with a bilateral craniectomy. On the night of September 24, 2008, I took the eight-minute ambulance ride from the hospital to Madonna.

To give you an idea of the condition I was in when I arrived at Madonna, I had been off the ventilator for less than a week, but my oxygen levels were good. I was becoming a little more responsive each day, opening my eyes more, turning my head towards voices, and responding to some requests. It took three people to move me out of the bed and into a chair. My head was misshapen because pieces of skull had been removed on both sides.

In scrolling through a DVD of home videos my dad took in the summer and fall of 2008, the action moves from ball games and birthday parties to me sitting on the bed in my room at Madonna next to my Grandpa John. The injury's impact is shockingly evident when watching my Grandpa help me lift my head to look at the camera. I moaned in obvious pain, and my eyes look confused and sad. It was the first video my dad had taken since my injury.

I had a long road ahead of me.

★ ★ ★ ★ ★

Waking up to the reality that your life has changed forever sucks. And that was rehab for me—day after day of pain and not being able to communicate what I wanted or needed or was afraid of or worried about. I couldn't even ask questions about what was happening to me. I could only respond to yes/no questions by giving a thumbs up with my left hand.

But I was fortunate. My mom was able to be with me constantly at Madonna, and the rest of my family visited often. I saw other patients who were far from their homes and rarely had family or friends with them. I had tons of visitors and support from my church and community. Father Sean Kilcawley, our parish priest, visited me every day. I also saw Father Stephen Cooney, the priest at Madonna, and Father Casey Porada, the hospital priest, who came to see me in rehab. Father Porada always had a daily riddle. I liked that. I looked forward to his visits; Father Porada would come and talk with me and give me a blessing. His riddles, talks, and blessings were just what I needed to give me the strength to get through the day. I had so many visitors that sometimes my family had to turn people away so I could get some rest. Ten days after my injury, Marc Bailey, a good family friend, created a Caring Bridge Journal. It is a personal online website used to share health information with family and friends. He or my mom would share updates to keep everyone informed on my progress.

My room at Madonna had a large south-facing window and space for my bed, a recliner, and a couch where my mom slept every night. Two of my favorite items in the room were the crucifix that hung above the window and the whiteboard where we counted down the days to my goal: being home for Christmas. The walls and shelves quickly filled with signs, cards, letters, and mementos from around the country. I had lots of signed University of Nebraska football memorabilia because my uncles Justin and Jordan were on the team at the time. I had a signed football and book from Tony Dungy, who was then coach of the NFL's Indianapolis Colts. I received a baseball signed by the New York Yankees and a football helmet signed by the Texas Longhorns. Heisman Trophy winner Eric Crouch, who played for the Huskers, sent me an autographed football.

The first few days at Madonna were mainly testing to establish a baseline so we could formulate a game plan for my rehabilitation. Holly Schifsky was my team leader. She had three boys of her own and had been a college athlete like my parents. She was a good fit for our family. Holly had read my records from the hospital: multiple hemorrhages within the brain, a large vessel rupture, diffuse axonal injuries (tearing in the nerve fibers that happens when the brain moves inside the skull after an injury), and downward pressure on my brain stem that caused injuries to other parts of my brain. I was very thin and had lost a lot of blood. Holly knew I had lots of challenges ahead. Knowing my medical history, she was ready to meet me and discover the strengths we could build on.

"I walked up to your bedside and took a minute to look at you and just marvel at the medical miracle that you were because this is not something that a lot of people would have survived," Holly said.

She said my name, and I turned my head. Holly asked me to give her a sign that I could hear her. I wiggled the fingers on my left hand. She asked me to move my legs. I tried. They started to shake. Then Holly surprised both my mom and me. She said I was going to take a shower. I hadn't had a shower since my injury.

Now, I'm a twelve-year-old boy just hitting puberty, so I was not too excited about my mom and this lady I had just met giving me a shower. But my entire time at Madonna, Holly, the nurses, and my family were very respectful and worked hard to preserve my dignity as much as possible. Still, it was no fun and was made even worse because I had to wear my helmet. I hated that helmet! Until doctors replaced the skull flaps taken out of my head, I had to wear a helmet to protect my brain whenever I was out of bed.

My mom and Holly sat me up and put my helmet on. They put me in a shower chair and gently washed me off with a sponge. It took about an hour. When I got stronger, Dad took over helping me in the shower. As uncomfortable as I was, that shower was the first normal thing I'd done in almost three weeks. Normal is good when recovering from an injury.

We settled into a routine. My mom would wake up and prepare for the day before it was time to get me up. I had physical therapy, speech therapy, and occupational therapy each day. They would bring us a schedule the night before. The days started early. Sometimes, I would have occupational therapy or speech therapy during breakfast to work on things like holding a spoon or swallowing. I was getting most of my nourishment through my feeding tube but would have light meals and snacks. My first 'real food' was chocolate ice cream on October 13. After the first tiny bite, the speech therapist working with me asked if I liked it. I gave a big thumbs-up!

I was not a typical patient. This was a critical point in time that, in many ways, my family had been preparing decades for. My grandfather, John Makovicka, earned his degree in physical therapy from the Mayo Clinic in Rochester, Minnesota, and was one of the first licensed physical therapists in Nebraska. My mom and two of my uncles, Joel and Jordan, followed in their dad's footsteps and became PTs. My Uncle Justin is an orthopedic surgeon. Plus, Michael Karel, one of the coaches on the sidelines when I got hurt, is a physician assistant and my mom's cousin. It blows me away that all these people with specialized training were in place, ready to help me.

Like any rehab hospital, Madonna had rules about having only qualified people transfer and lift patients. My mom was qualified to help me use the bathroom, but not everyone there was convinced of that. My family understands how to strengthen muscles. My therapies with the Madonna staff would end at four or five in the afternoon. My family did not want me to just lie in bed all night and then start over the next morning, so my grandpa would stretch me and work with me every evening. At first, it was just sitting me on the edge of the bed and working on head control, like Dad captured on the first video he took of me at Madonna. Without my skull flaps, I could not sense where my head was in space, so Grandpa worked with me on lifting my head. Later, Madonna let us use a room at the end of the hall where Grandpa would stretch my large muscles on a mat table. My family also spent hours going up and down halls with me, helping me re-learn how to walk.

Six days after I arrived at Madonna, I got my trach out. I also could now stand for fifteen minutes with maximum assistance. On Friday, October 10, thirty-four days after my injury, I wrote my first word. With help from my occupational therapist, I spelled B-A-S-K-E-T-B-A-L-L with my left hand. It was an emotional moment! Mom wrote about that day and the days that followed in my Caring Bridge Journal:

When I look back to those first days, I can see how far we have come. The images and sounds of the initial days will be forever etched in my heart and memory.

Derek continues to make progress. Sometimes, the daily progress is so minimal that it is easier to look back a week to make the comparison. This past week Derek has continued to gain improvement in his left arm and hand. He is able to answer yes/no questions with his thumb on this hand and can now also wave. We have also developed a way for him to communicate by holding up a certain number with his fingers. He does continue to make sounds but has not yet mastered the skill of voice. We are waiting anxiously until that day.

Derek continues to take baby steps, and all his doctors have told us, "This is a marathon and not a sprint." Even though I have repeatedly told them that I am a SPRINTER! No one is listening! We all know that our journey is just beginning, and it is so hard not to look back at our life before September 6, but this is the path that has been chosen for our family, and we will continue to take one day at a time and rejoice that it is one day and not minute-to-minute as we had lived the first days.

We all wish that we could go back . . . somehow turn back the hands of time, but we are here now, and we are determined to fight till the end. I can't look ahead; the road seems too long and the outcome so unknown. I have to stay focused and believe that we will all make it. Our family will never look at life the same, and we will forever be changed because of something that happened so quickly without warning. I guess that is why it is better for us not to know the plan that God has in store for each of us. We may never know the reason that this tragedy happened, but we will trust that He will continue to guide us into the future.

On October 3, 2008, nine days after I arrived at Madonna and nearly four weeks after my injury, I turned thirteen years old. I don't remember this birthday, but my family recalls celebrating in a lounge area near the cafeteria. This became the place for gatherings, including my birthday, Brenden's first birthday on October 16, Dad's and Connor's birthdays on October 29, Trevor's birthday on November 1, and lots of other family get togethers.

Though all my brothers spent time with me at Madonna, Brenden was there the most. My Grandma Connie was staying at our house to help my dad and brothers. Some days she brought Brenden to hang out with Mom and me. Brenden would crawl up on the bed and "help" me with my exercises. One of the big reasons I wanted to leave Heaven and stay with my family when Jesus gave me the choice was so I could see Brenden grow up.

It is difficult to explain how grueling therapy was. I had to relearn everything! How to swallow, how to hold a spoon, how to sit, how to stand, how to walk—it was physically excruciating and emotionally exhausting. And progress was painfully slow.

Though my muscle control was like an infant's, my mind was still sharp. On October 22, I started going to The Learning Center (TLC) at Madonna. The room was at the end of a hallway and was quieter than the gym. It is easy for a brain injury patient to be overstimulated, and it is hard to stay on task when a lot is going on. At TLC, I met Nova, who would be my teacher. She realized that I was still intelligent even though my communication was limited. She treated me like the seventh grader I was. That first day, we did multiplication and reading comprehension. I was glad to get back to schoolwork so I could stay up with my class. A new goal was to return to Malcolm Junior/Senior High and start eighth grade with them in August 2009.

So, I added time in TLC with Nova to my daily therapy schedule. In the first week at Madonna, Mom realized that if she took me to the gym or treatment rooms rather than waiting for aides to come and get me, I could spend more time doing therapies. Mom logged miles taking me around Madonna in my wheelchair. We even found some time for extra sessions with Nova or time in the gym with just Mom and me working on the Upper Body Ergometers (UBEs), which are like bikes you operate with your arms. I used my left arm on the UBE. My right arm continued to be a concern. It was probably most impacted by the brain injury. The first sign something was wrong in the football game was my right arm went limp, and I fumbled the ball. When I arrived at Madonna, my right arm was flaccid and hung at my side. As my brain activity increased, my arm got spastic, and then the muscles in my bicep and elbow started contracting and pulling up tight, so my hand was up against my face. On October 21, I had my first Botox injections to help reduce the tone in my right upper extremities.

My days were full, and after supper, Grandpa would arrive, and we'd begin to stretch and work on rebuilding those muscles that had atrophied while I was in the ICU. As an athlete, I had worked hard before. Remember all those workouts I did in the summer? They were nothing compared to the daunting regimen I had now. This was more difficult than any two-a-days, and the stakes were much higher. In many ways, the work we did determined my quality of life for the years ahead.

You would think with all that therapy and stretching, day after day, I would have slept well at night. But no. Nights were awful. That was when I tried to process everything. It was the time when I experienced the pain. When Jesus offered me the choice to be in Heaven or remain with my family, I had no idea what that would be like. Those nights were especially when I started to figure it out. And I prayed. At night I would pour out my thoughts to Jesus and Mary. I would not have survived that dark time without them.

I found a place of solace at Madonna in a small side chapel. I attended daily mass in the main chapel, which was spacious and quiet with a vaulted ceiling—rays from the sun streamed through the skylight and fell on the crucifix above the altar. But the place I loved most was a small chapel off to the right where a blue and amber stained-glass window backlit a statue of the

Blessed Virgin Mary. The stations of the cross were depicted on the walls. I would place my wheelchair directly in front of the tabernacle, and I would spend a good amount of time each day in that chapel directly in front of Jesus.

* * * * *

In early November, I got sick with bouts of fever and vomiting. I returned to the hospital for a CT scan to see if my brain was swelling again. Fortunately, no acute changes showed up. Doctors adjusted my medications and food volume, and I returned to Madonna, where I continued to get stronger and even began to initiate voluntary movements. And I made my family happy when I smiled. It's astounding the impact a smile had on our hope after so many days of fighting hopelessness.

"He cannot voluntarily smile, but he can elicit a smile when he sees his brothers or hears something funny," Mom said. "His smile warms your heart. It is so Derek—that big, crooked smile that lights up his entire face. His eyes just shine."

On Monday, November 17, I took the eight-minute ride back to the hospital so doctors could place the two bone flaps stored in my abdominal wall tissue back in my skull.

I remember very clearly the night before that surgery because my brothers, uncles, aunts, and a handful of my friends came to see me in the hospital. This was a scary surgery, and it was uncertain if I would make it through. Father Kilcawley gave me my last rights and prayed over me. I had last rites so many times following my injury that I can't even count them.

The surgery lasted about four hours and went smoothly. I had four incisions, two on my head and two on my abdomen. The long incisions on my head ran from my hairline in front down each side of my skull to the base. They were held together with staples. Dad took another video after the surgery. The good news: my head was no longer misshapen, and I did not have to wear that stupid helmet anymore. The bad news: all those staples had to be taken out. I don't know how many there were, but I do remember it hurt pretty bad and made a bloody mess when they removed them two weeks later.

They kept me in a medically induced coma the first day after surgery to keep the pressure in my brain from increasing. I spent six days in ICU and had lots of nausea and vomiting, but all the scans looked good. I was groggy for several days. It can take longer for the anesthetic to wear off after a traumatic brain injury. A week after surgery, I moved to a regular hospital room. I was still feeling sick and vomited up all the barium they gave me when they tried to do a stomach X-ray. When my digestive system finally settled down, I went back to Madonna, weak but ready to get back to work on my goal of being home by Christmas.

In all the weeks since my injury, my mom had only been back to our home a few times. She spent a few hours at home on family birthdays. After I was more stable, she spent a few nights at home, and my dad or grandpa would stay with me at Madonna. My mom is one of the strongest people I know. Reflecting on the weeks after my injury, Mom said it was difficult to suddenly not be able to make decisions for her son. Doctors, hospitals, and insurance companies now had a say on what I could do and where I could go. My parents could not drive me in their car or even take me home for a visit. It was frustrating and complicated. She said later that she really did not know how we got through that time other than just getting up each day and doing what needed to be done.

The first two weeks after the skull flap surgery were rough, but I regained strength and reached some milestones. On Sunday, December 7, Dad and Uncle Joel were teasing me and making me laugh. Mom asked if I wanted them to stop, and I yelled, "Yeah!" Everyone in the room erupted in laughter, shouts, and tears. It was my first word in three months! Later that night, before bed, I said, "Love you, Mom."

"I had waited so long to hear him say 'Mom.' I think it was even better than when he said it as an infant," Mom said.

And I took my first step one evening in the hallway. Grandpa and Dad were helping me. Mom was there, along with Scott Amen, one of the

Malcolm High School football coaches. Grandpa decided to put a band under my foot to help me remember the pattern of lifting and stepping. And it clicked. I got the extensor reflex going, and I lifted my foot and set it back down again on my own for the first time. Dad says he can still go to the exact spot in the hallway at Madonna where it happened. I was months away from walking on my own, but I had taken the first step!

I do not have many fond memories of those three months in rehab. I experienced intense physical and emotional pain. I often held my hand to my head to relieve the constant headaches. I was trapped in a body that I could not make work the way I wanted. I had a million thoughts and questions running through my mind and very limited ways to share them with anyone else. I do know this: Grandpa John wouldn't let me give up. He worked with me every night, stretching me beyond belief. He was certain I would walk and knew how to help retrain my muscles. He saved me.

★ ★ ★ ★ ★

My mom remembers that when I was in the ICU, she prayed that I would just live for one more minute, then for five more minutes. And when I did live, she realized she wanted more. She wanted me to come home. She wanted me to walk. She wanted me to talk. She wanted more for me. She still does.

"As a mom, we always want to protect our child and help them when they are suffering, and this continues to be a difficult and emotional journey for me," Mom said. "I would love to be able to pick Derek up and hold him and make everything better like I have done so many times before. But this is so different, and it is hard for me to even understand what he is going through. I know how hard it is for all of us and can't imagine how hard it is for him. He is very cognitive of his situation."

On Friday, November 7, the nurse and my mom were trying to figure out what was wrong with me. They knew I was in pain. They asked where and I typed H-E-A-R-T. They thought I was having chest pain, but my heart hurt—it was sad and broken.

CHAPTER FOUR

Three weeks before I was born, my parents and grandparents took a road trip to East Lansing, Michigan, to watch my uncles play football. They mapped out hospitals every fifty miles along the route in case my mom went into labor. But I waited for a bye week.

I arrived on Tuesday, October 3, 1995, at 3:50 p.m. I was the first child born to Jennifer and Royce Ruth and the first grandchild and nephew. I was a perfectly healthy baby who weighed in at a robust nine pounds eight ounces. My parents had just moved out of an apartment into a yellow, two-story house in the Highlands, a new housing area in northwest Lincoln, Nebraska. It had a big backyard. My room was on the second floor. On Sunday, October 22, nineteen days after I was born, I was baptized at Saint Mary's Catholic Church in Lincoln. My uncle and aunt, Jeff and Tracy Makovicka, are my godparents.

My mom's two youngest brothers were just six and seven years old when I was born. While they are technically my uncles, Justin and Jordan are more like older brothers. They did everything imaginable with me: held me, fed me, and played with me. I have looked up to them my entire life.

My dad is a financial advisor, and Mom is a physical therapist. When Mom went back to work, I went to a daycare owned by my great aunts Nancy and Jan. They spoiled me and every other kid who went to that daycare.

Being born into my family means being born into sports. I didn't slow my parents down much. We went to every Nebraska Cornhusker home football game the rest of the season. When I was just a little more than two weeks old, my parents traveled to Colorado for an away game. My mom dropped me off in Kearney, Nebraska, and her good friend from college watched me. When I was not quite three months old, I joined the family entourage on a trip to Tempe, Arizona, for the Fiesta Bowl. As soon as I was old enough to move around, I gravitated to balls: footballs, baseballs, and basketballs. Some of my younger brothers were interested in farm machinery and trucks, but for me, it was always about balls.

Just shy of a year old, I began to talk. Really talk. I talked a lot in long, complete sentences. People always thought I was much older than I was because I was tall and very talkative. I was also onery and could find my way into mischief. I always liked to be active and was never one for watching much TV. My parents got me into gymnastics when I was two years old to help channel some of my energy.

I gained a brother in June 1998 when I was two-and-a-half years old. I immediately felt an unbelievable amount of love for Corbin. I had gained a new best friend and responsibility. I knew I had to protect him and show him how to live. I wanted Corbin to look up to me just like I looked up to Justin and Jordan. I took the responsibility of being a big brother very seriously. Three other brothers would join our family. Connor is four years younger than me, Trevor is eight years younger, and Brenden is twelve. Each of their births greatly impacted me, but Brenden's birth changed me. I can't explain exactly why, but I felt more mature after he was born—I felt an even more special responsibility for him. When Jesus gave me a choice between Heaven and Earth, Brenden was the one I thought of.

Life in the Highlands was idyllic for a kid. So many young families lived in the neighborhood, and I had lots of friends. That was when I first realized I was a leader. Kids looked up to me and would follow me around. One neighborhood mom called me the Pied Piper. I tried to lead by example and include everyone.

Just before I was five, I began attending preschool at North American Martyrs Catholic School, which was attached to the church my family and I belonged to. I went to school three half-days each week. I was nervous the first few days, but I was always talking, and it didn't take long for me to make friends. It was easy to go to school because I had a teacher I really liked, plus she liked me! When Christmas rolled around that year, my preschool class had a play about the Nativity. I was a shepherd. On Christmas Day that year, I remember getting baseball equipment, including a bat, glove, batting gloves, and baseball pants.

The Nebraska winters did not faze my brothers or me. We loved the snow! My brothers and I built snow forts and had snowball fights. We tested our endurance by seeing who could be outside the longest without any clothes. And we would play football in the backyard. The competition between Corbin and me could get intense. We don't always get along, but my brothers are my best friends. We always have each other's backs.

In the spring of 2001, I started on my baseball journey alongside many of the teammates I'd play with my entire career. We played in a recreational league and beat every team by several runs. We played fifteen games throughout the months of June and July. After that season, I knew I loved baseball.

In August, we moved to an acreage near Malcolm, Nebraska, about twelve miles northwest of Lincoln. It was a tough move because I was leaving so many neighborhood friends. But I was excited to have more room and freedom. I had to decide which school to attend that fall. My two choices were to stay at North American Martyrs or go to Malcolm Public Schools. I chose Malcolm, which was closer to our new home. It took me a while to get used to my new school. It was smaller, and the religious aspect was not part of the public school. I missed that.

One of the lures of the acreage was our parents' promise to get us a dog. In the spring, we got a puppy! We picked out a big black lab and named him Bear. We taught Bear to play fetch, wrestled with him, and had all kinds of adventures together.

Organized sports were becoming a bigger part of my life. In the winter of 2001, I attended an instructional basketball camp. That summer, I played in the same baseball league. In January 2003, I played in a three-on-three basketball league that combined games with instruction. In March, I played micro soccer. I didn't like soccer at all! I was too physically aggressive to play that game.

As important as sports were in our lives, my parents taught me from the beginning that faith and family come first. In March 2004, I received my second and third sacraments of the Catholic Church. I had my first penance, better known as confession, at the beginning of March to take away all of my sins so I could receive the body and blood of Jesus Christ in my first communion later that month. I recited one of the readings during that mass. My first communion was a monumental day for me and my family—powerful and life-changing because I was now in communion with the Church. Holy Communion, for me, was like a rite of passage; I was now spiritually mature enough to understand the importance of what I was receiving. Ever since that day, I have found great peace when I receive Jesus in the Eucharist.

I was not a kid who was publicly outgoing about my Catholic faith, even though my life revolved around it. I grew up wearing a cross around my neck, but I always had it beneath my shirt. I always prayed before my meals at school, but I would not make the sign of the cross visible to anyone. Instead, I would make the sign of the cross in my head, or I would make it look like a regular activity so no one would notice. If people did see me, they would make fun of me, but that didn't bother me because I knew I was doing the right thing.

School was easy for me, and I always did well academically. Grades were important as well, and I made sure I finished my homework every night. Math was my favorite subject. I was not always good at showing my work, but I almost always came up with the correct answers.

Like many firstborns, I am Type A, and that started to show more as I got older. I'm meticulous and set routines. I have always been very neat and cared about my appearance, though I do pop my knuckles and chew my fingernails. I'm also very driven and competitive. Yeah, I liked to have fun and joke around, but I knew there was a certain place and time for that. Did I give 100 percent in every area of my life? You better believe I did, and that paid off for me. If I was on time for an event or activity, that was late in my mind. Ten minutes early is on time. I tried to be the first to the top in everything I did. Persistence and discipline are aspects of life that I am good at. To this day, respect has played a major part in my life. I strive to be respected and respectful.

When I was eleven years old, I received the sacrament of confirmation. I chose Michael as my confirmation name after Saint Michael the Arch Angel. After I was confirmed, I began to pray the most Holy Rosary daily. When I found out that my mom was pregnant again, I began offering a decade of the Rosary for each one of my family members. A decade is a part of the Rosary; the Rosary consists of five decades. During each decade, you recite ten Hail Mary prayers. Each decade is preceded by one Our Father and followed by one Glory Be prayer. I would offer one decade for my parents and then the other four decades for each of my brothers. I would pray the most Holy Rosary as well as do push-ups and sit-ups before getting into bed for the night.

My grandparents were staying with us on the evening of September 4, 2008. Grandpa was rocking Brenden to sleep in his room, while the rest of us were supposed to be getting ready for bed. My room was right across the hall, and Grandpa could see the light coming from under my door. He laid Brenden down and stormed across the hall to scold me. When he opened the door, he found me on my knees praying.

Two days later, I was injured on the football field.

CHAPTER FIVE

The morning of Saturday, December 20, 2008, I looked out my rehabilitation hospital room window to see a pretty, light snow falling from the sky. That day marked the fifteenth week I had been in hospitals between Bryan LGH and Madonna. It had been an extremely long and gruesome period, going through multiple brain surgeries, coming out of my coma, and beginning the hard work of relearning almost everything. The thing that was different about this day, though, was that I was finally getting released from the rehabilitation hospital to go back to living at home just in time for Christmas!

From the moment I woke up in the hospital, my focus had been on going home. We made it our family goal for me to be home by Christmas. Not everyone supported that desire. Some people thought it was pushing too fast and it would be too hard on my family and me. It was a big decision. Because of insurance regulations, once I left inpatient rehab, I could not go back. Even though my mom was with me most of the time at Madonna, and I saw my dad and brothers, I missed being at home, hanging out with them, and eating together. I missed my family. So, despite the

31

challenges, my parents understood how important it was for our family to be back together and chose to take me home in December.

We counted down the days on the whiteboard in my room at Madonna, and I worked hard to reach the milestones that would make the transition possible. I was allowed to go home for four hours to celebrate the Feast of St. Nicholas on Saturday, December 6. My parents asked if I could visit home on a few other occasions, but that was the first time we got approval. Our house had to be inspected—even the car I would travel home in had to be approved—and my parents had to be trained on how to transport me. That visit also allowed my parents to see what modifications our home would need before I returned for good. On that trip, my dad and grandpa had to carry me through the front door. A video of my visit shows me sitting in my wheelchair in our living room, surrounded by excited brothers opening gifts. I appeared dazed but happy as my brothers helped me unwrap my new Nike shorts.

While I was doing physical, occupational, and speech therapy to retrain my brain and body, family and close friends were spending evenings and weekends transforming our garage into a mini therapy/workout room and making some modifications to our house. They installed a wheelchair lift. I could roll my chair onto the electric lift, and it would raise me to the level of the back door that went from our garage into our house. They also modified our shower and installed safety bars in our bathroom.

In the garage, they set up a mat table—a big square table a foot or two off the ground for stretching. They installed another PT platform table that folded down and set up cages with free weights, an Airdyne bike, a NuStep recumbent cross trainer, and a leg press. When I was home for good, I would have everything I needed to stretch and workout.

It was difficult to return to Madonna after that short visit, but I had two more weeks of inpatient rehab. Those final days seemed to drag. At last, it was December 20, and I was finally going home. I have vivid memories of that day.

Mom and Dad wheeled me out of the rehabilitation hospital and got me into our family car. Because I had so little strength, Dad basically had to lift me out of the wheelchair and put me in the car. He buckled me in super tight, making sure I would not move during the ride home. Mom drove, taking her time to make sure the ride was as smooth as possible.

When we pulled into our driveway, I felt an unbelievable amount of relief. Nothing can even come close to describing what it is like living in a hospital room for more than three months. Mom pulled into the garage, and Dad helped me transfer from the car into my wheelchair. I used the wheelchair lift to reach the back door. I was not walking when I went home. I had taken some steps but still relied on my wheelchair to get around.

When I finally got into our home, things were arranged differently than I remembered. Rather than being spread out, the couches and loveseat were in the corner of the living room to make room for an air mattress and a hospital bed. I would use the hospital bed for the time being because I could not get up the stairs to my room. My parents slept on the air mattress to be close to me.

Mom and Dad helped me out of the wheelchair and onto the air mattress to let me stretch out and take everything in. It was an emotional time for me. After a few minutes, my four younger brothers came into the room to talk to me and have some normal interaction for the first time in months. My baby brother, Brenden, was now walking and talking nonstop. He would run into the side of the air mattress and bounce off, which he thought was a game, plus he was also trying to get on the mattress with me.

My parents eventually put him up on the mattress beside me. He kept yelling, "D! D!" and smiling. Being with my baby brother at that moment was not very easy for me from the emotional side of things. I had missed his first steps and his first words. Brenden took his first steps in the hospital where I underwent my initial surgeries and began talking weeks later while I was at Madonna. Brenden tried to take his first steps at home, but Grandma and his other caregivers kept pushing him down until they could get him to the hospital, where my parents could see him walk for the first time.

That moment on the mattress motivated me because I did not want my baby brother to remember me as I was at that moment.

Later, we went into the kitchen. I sat in a chair with a tray on it, kind of like a highchair, and had lunch. I still had my feeding tube, and the only things I could eat by mouth were liquids, soups, and baby food. That first day, I had soup from Panera and some sort of baby food. My grandma fed me while my parents stood/sat beside me, making sure I was stable.

I was extremely worn out by the move home, so after lunch, Dad carried me to the hospital bed for a nap. Later that evening, we watched a movie together. I had a little more to eat, then went to bed for the night.

Before Christmas, I had a few days to readjust to home and our new life. My parents got me up in the middle of each night to feed me. Most of my nutrients, medications, and even water came through my feeding tube. I remember my mouth and lips were so dry!

My being home also meant my grandma got to go home. She and Grandpa had rushed to the hospital directly from the Husker football game the day I was hurt. She stayed at the hospital for the first three or four days, still wearing her Husker gear. Everyone in Nebraska wears red on game day. When she did leave the hospital, she went straight to our house to help take care of my brothers. Now, she had a break to be at home for a few days. When I started day rehab in January, she moved back in with us until Easter.

We had our traditional family Christmas dinner on December 24: prime rib, potatoes, broccoli casserole, and shrimp. I was hardly able to eat and was in a great deal of pain. Mom modified a little bit of food for me, but not being able to fully indulge in Christmas dinner was rough. I shed a few tears. Everything was frustrating, and I was tired of the tube and not being able to eat like I had before. I also hated that my brothers had to see me like that. I was supposed to be the big brother who protected them and paved the way for them. Now I was eating baby food.

Then Christmas Day came, and my family and I went to Christmas mass at North American Martyrs. We sat in the front row of the church because that row had a spot for a wheelchair. As Father Sean Kilcawley offered Christmas mass, emotion flowed through my body. I felt incredibly thankful that I could go to mass at my home parish and celebrate Christmas with my parish family. The North American Martyrs family is incredibly close to one another. They had been so supportive of my family and me and prayed so many prayers for us.

After mass, my family and I went home, and we had my grandparents, uncles, and aunts over to celebrate Christmas, and even Father Kilcawley showed up. My brothers got a basketball hoop, and Brenden got a toy tractor that he pushed around the living room, over and around the rest of the presents. I got a new Air Jordan sweatshirt and some slippers. Once we finished opening gifts, we relaxed on the main level of our house. The last couple of months had taken a physical and emotional toll, not just on me but my entire family. But for now, we were home together. The next phase of rehab could wait until the new year.

★ ★ ★ ★ ★

After just three or four weeks at home, I started making significant progress. On January 10, 2009, I took ten steps with no assistance! It turns out that being at home with my family was a vital part of my recovery. My brothers and I were figuring out ways to communicate, but it wasn't long before we were teasing each other, getting on each other's nerves, and even fighting—basically just being brothers.

I was now going to outpatient rehab each day at Madonna. My mom went with me four days a week, and Dad went with me on Wednesdays to give her a break. I followed much of the same schedule I had when I was inpatient. I had physical therapy, occupational therapy, and speech therapy, and they added aqua therapy. It was my last session of the day, and I was not a fan. I continued to work with Nova Adams on my schoolwork. I still planned to join my class back at Malcolm Junior/Senior High in the fall. Nova was creative and made schoolwork fun. That spring, she put together a March Madness bracket for the NCAA basketball tournament. She did not know anything about basketball but knew that I was a huge fan of the North Carolina Tar Heels. She got lots of the people at Madonna to participate in the bracket, then put me to work figuring out percentages, win probabilities, and other statistics. North Carolina started the tournament as the top seed in the South Regional, which made one of my therapists, Jen Sullivan, and me really happy. Jen was also a big Tar Heel fan. North Carolina made it to the finals and beat Michigan State 89-72. It was one of the highlights of the year!

By late January, I was walking 100 feet with a contact guard assist. That means someone was with me to help steady me, but I was walking on my own. I was using my wheelchair less and less. At the end of one long day, my legs were shaking, and my therapists wanted me to get in the wheelchair to go to the gym for my last session. No way! I was not going to use that chair! I was tired, but I was determined to walk to the gym. And I did! I always knew I would walk and eventually run. People think that the injury changed me, and yes, it did in a way. But I still had many of the same goals I did prior to the injury. I just had no idea what to expect and what I would have to go through to get back to living the life I wanted.

And I wanted to be back in my own room. The hospital bed did not stay in our living room very long. As soon as I could go up the steps with help from my parents, it was out of there, and I was upstairs, back in my own bed. At first, my parents put an alarm on my door so they would know when I got up at night. They were afraid I would stumble or even fall down the stairs. As I gained strength and got steadier on my feet, we all learned to trust my ability, and the alarm went away.

Being home was the medicine I needed. But being out of the hospital and back in my environment also forced me to face reality. I was not the same. My life was not the same and never would be. These sobering truths were just starting to sink in.

My right arm and speech were some of the biggest hurdles, and we focused on those a lot during outpatient therapy. I was still doing Botox injections to help relax the muscles in my right arm and hand. One of the therapies I did was kind of fun. Dad brought in a bucket of baseballs, and we practiced the grips needed to throw certain pitches. I had to correct him on some of his grips.

After my long days at Madonna, I worked out in my garage gym. Grandpa still came to stretch and work with me on building strength for about an hour and a half each evening. I was learning that it would take extra effort to function independently and do things that most people can do without thinking. As I pressed my parents and doctors for more information about my injury and expectations, the truth was sometimes very painful. But I was also aware of how very fortunate I was.

In late January, Mom drove me to the doctor's office for an appointment. She pulled into an accessible parking space near the front door.

"Am I handicapped?" I asked her.

She said she parked there so I didn't have to walk so far. I asked her not to use the sticker anymore and to leave those spots for people who need them more than I do.

At day rehab, I saw people who were worse off than I was. I was an adolescent boy who had injured the part of the brain that deals with emotional expression, so I had my share of mood swings, but I always had compassion for the other patients.

"You had a really severe injury," Holly, who was still my occupational therapist, said, "yet you would look around in the gym and show a lot of empathy to the people around you. You would ask me if other people were going to be okay."

I rarely complained to other people, but I was discouraged and frustrated much of the time. I was used to working hard and putting in extra effort. But I was also used to seeing results. In sports, my training and extra workouts led to tangible improvements in speed and skill. Now, I was putting in two or three times the work and often not seeing much, if any, return.

I was incredibly discouraged about my speech. I was using my tongue as a postural stabilizer to help with my balance, so I had a hard time closing my mouth, and I drooled all the time. I hated that! I always had to have a towel with me. They let me do some of my schoolwork and therapies in kind of a private side room where not as many people could see me struggle but I still wanted to be perceived as capable and as a leader. Therapy was grueling, and I would get mad at myself for not being able to make my body do what I wanted. Sometimes, I'd send pegs from the pegboard flying or hit my hand on the table in frustration. Then, I'd take a minute to shake it off and get back to work.

I got to visit school. Nova and Holly wanted to see the space and figure out what accommodations I would need when I returned to classes in the fall. Some of my friends met us at the door, and we walked around with them. It was good to be back, but it was also painful to realize what I had missed and see that life had gone on without me. I wore jeans that day; it was the first time Nova and Holly had seen me in anything other than athletic wear. We talked about which areas of the school would be challenging in terms of mobility, where I would eat lunch, etc. The thought of going back to school kept me motivated on some very dark days.

My friends really helped me that year. Two or three friends even came to some of my outpatient therapy with me a few times. It's true what they say: It takes a team to get you through the tough times.

CHAPTER SIX

Y"ou don't realize how much people will support and get behind you until you experience a tragedy. From the one hundred-plus people who came to the hospital for a prayer vigil the day after my injury, to those who supported my family during my recovery with meals, babysitting, laundry, and so many other practical things, to those who organized dinners and other fundraisers, Team Derek was strong!

We were surrounded by love and prayers from so many people. Friends organized ongoing prayer groups to lift my petitions to Jesus. People made black and blue wristbands with my number twenty-two on them and donated the proceeds to my family. At Malcolm Public Schools and throughout Lincoln and Omaha, kids wore blue athletic socks in my honor with one sock up, and the other sock pulled down. That was the way I wore my socks when I played.

In the spring, two of my mom's friends organized a big fundraising effort as part of the annual Lincoln Marathon. Diane Kluthe and Teresa Bruggeman recruited people to run or walk the marathon in my honor. Seventy-five people, including several of my therapists and nurses from Madonna, signed up. They wore blue Team Derek shirts that said, "Distance with determination." Another two hundred people bought the T-shirts to help support our family. Many of these fans were at water stations and along the marathon route to cheer on Team Derek.

While Team Derek was training, I worked on strength, endurance, and stability so I could finish the race with them. The night before the marathon, we had a Team Derek pasta feed.

The marathon was on Sunday, May 3, 2009. It was a beautiful sunny day with temperatures in the upper fifties at race time. The start and finish lines were in the horseshoe drive on the east side of Memorial Stadium. We joined members of Team Derek to walk around the horseshoe and cross the finish line together. I amazed everyone when I ran the last few yards with a huge smile on my face.

Team Derek buoyed my spirits and inspired me to persevere and continue putting in the long, hard hours at therapy. To this day, people continue to support, challenge, and pray for me. My brothers have honored me throughout their athletic careers by wearing number twenty-two.

CHAPTER
SEVEN

Athletics were an ordinary, everyday thing for me. I loved the adrenaline rush I would get when I was competing. I played every sport at the highest level possible and thrived on success.

The first sport I really enjoyed was baseball. I had to play two years of t-ball and coach-pitch before baseball really began for me. In 2004, I made the Lincoln Sox, a select baseball team out of Lincoln. Before tryouts came in July, I still played recreational baseball. After each game, several coaches would ask me to try out for their team. Practice for the select team began in mid-August. I was also playing in a baseball league in Omaha through the Strike Zone. At the time, the Strike Zone was the premiere baseball center in Nebraska. We played games every Saturday throughout the fall.

I played almost every position on the field, but the place I liked playing the most was shortstop. In the winter of 2005, my dad would take me to the Strike Zone indoor facility for private lessons. Those lessons lasted a little over an hour, and I worked on every area of my game: pitching, hitting, and fielding. Dad would videotape those private lessons, and at night, when I was lying in bed, I would visualize myself doing great things on the ball diamond. People say you find your first true love early in life, something, or someone you cannot live without; mine was baseball.

That winter, Dad put a batting cage in the shed behind our house. We also had a basketball hoop in the shed. I would spend hours in the shed practicing and training, hitting baseballs and shooting baskets. I called the shed my office because that was where I went to work.

In the middle of February, I began to practice for the Lincoln Sox and absolutely loved it. Games started in late March. Our team uniforms were long black socks, white pinstripe pants with a black belt, a black vest with the team logo on the left chest, red and black henleys to go under the team vest, and a red hat with a black bill with the logo on the front. I was very superstitious when I played the game. When I took the field, I would always hop over the base chalk and be the first one out on the diamond.

I played almost every position because I was a versatile athlete, but I spent much of that season playing shortstop and batting in the two-hole, second in the lineup. I wore number two, and I threw and batted right-handed. That season, our pitching rotation was not very deep. We would usually win the first couple of games in pool play, then when tournament games came around on Sunday, we would be out of pitching by the championship game and end up getting beat.

In July, right after the state tournament, our team went to a national baseball tournament in Saint Louis, Missouri. My teammates and I had a blast when we were off the diamond, but on the diamond, we made some memories that will be with us for the rest of our lives. The Lincoln Sox went three and one in pool play and were in the top bracket of the double-elimination tournament. In our final game, we got beat by a team from the South. It was an amazing experience playing teams from throughout the country.

Tryouts came around for the 2006 season, and we ended up losing four players and picking up two new ones. Watching those four players go their own way was tough, but that's the risk you take when you play at the top. In February, practice began at an indoor facility in Lincoln. At the same time, I was taking private pitching lessons at the University of Nebraska–Lincoln from Saul Soltero, director of the Nebraska Baseball Academy. I worked with Saul throughout that season.

That was the year I became a leader. I knew I had been given the gift to lead. I always led the warmups before practices and games. I would lead vocally and lead by example. My teammates came to expect that from me, and I took pride in being a leader. Games began in late March. During the year, I was moved up to lead-off batter. I liked hitting lead-off because the majority of the first pitches in games are fastballs, so I knew what to expect, and I always had the green light. That season concluded with a national tournament in Kansas City, Kansas.

When the 2007 season began in the middle of February, our team picked up two new players along with new uniforms. We got rid of the team vests and got dry-fit jerseys and new baseball pants that were completely white with a black stripe down the side. While we were taking batting practice in the batting cages, we each gave one another nicknames. My nickname was D-money, and it has been my nickname ever since. We won most of the tournaments we were in that season because we had a deep pitching rotation and were an all-around good team. I pitched a lot that season. I threw a four and two seam fastball and a circle changeup. My family did not allow me to throw a curveball because they did not want me to hurt my elbow at age eleven. I pitched out of the windup when no runners were on base because I felt my velocity was better. When there were base runners, I would always throw from the stretch. Another thing I used to do when I was pitching was to draw a line in the dirt in front of the pitching mound. I did that to lengthen my stride and to make sure I was following through.

I also had some good pick-off moves because I had quick feet. For example, when a runner was on first base, I would either step off the mound and throw the ball lightly over to first base to keep the runner honest or do a jump turn to first base. With a runner on second base, I would do the chair or spin move. Either of those pick-off moves was equally effective for me going to second.

In mid-June, Nebraska becomes a baseball state as The College World Series is held in Omaha. At that exact same time, my team would go to a tournament that was also in Omaha. Teams from across the country would play in the Road to Omaha tournament. We got second place that year, losing to a team from California in the championship game. In July, we played in another national tournament in Shawnee, Kansas. That season was our best season in terms of record.

★ ★ ★ ★ ★

In January 2006, I was asked to join a select basketball team, the Lincoln Blaze. The two coaches, Matt and Rick, scouted and watched me play a few rec basketball games. I was not competing at a high level because basketball really was not my sport. I mainly just played to keep in shape. After a game in late January, Matt and Rick approached me and asked if I would like to join their team. Unfortunately, it was the middle of the season, so I could only play in tournaments.

The Blaze played a high-tempo offense I loved. It was a run-and-gun game and we scored most of our points off fast breaks and turnovers. I played guard and scored some, but my main contribution was rebounding and lock-down defense. I would dive to the ground going after loose balls, and when I played defense, I would be right up on the opposing player in their face, and I would shut them down. The Blaze had two or three players who scored most of the points, so when I got a rebound, I would immediately get the ball to one of those players, and they would take off up court and make something happen.

I was officially part of the Blaze for the 2007 season. Practices began in early November and games later that month. I brought a certain toughness to the team. I was a tough-minded all-around athlete with a higher basketball IQ than many kids my age.

★ ★ ★ ★ ★

44

I was a very gifted athlete, and I enjoyed every single sport I competed in, but I had a special passion for the game of football. I loved to compete, and I especially showed it on the football field.

I began playing tackle football in fifth grade. I played middle linebacker on defense, and on offense I lined up at running back. When it came time for the two-minute offense, I would move to quarterback because I had a strong and accurate arm. I wore number twenty-two because my Uncle Jordan, who is just six years older than me, wore that number. I idolized Jordan and wanted to follow in his footsteps. When I was in fifth grade, he was a junior in high school and one of the top athletes in the state. We have a similar body makeup, and we also played the game alike, or at least I like to think so from what I witnessed firsthand when I would go watch him play in person every Friday night during the fall. My games were on Saturday or Sunday afternoons.

During football practice, I listened well, acted on the directions that were given, and asked great questions. I learned football at an early age, so when I asked why we were doing something a certain way, I knew that if I didn't understand it, the others for sure didn't get it. I always practiced hard and pushed myself, leading others to push themselves, too. I was patient, positive, encouraging, consistent, authentic, and humble. I was respectful and respected as a leader who helped and lifted up those around me who needed it.

When it came to football, I was intelligent and had a great understanding of the game, which led me to have a nose for the ball and an awareness of what was going on around me. I knew my role and the role of others, and I made good decisions. I was assignment-sound and dependable, plus I was a coach on the field.

"There wasn't anyone else on the field that knew what was coming next better than Derek," one of my teammates said. "Every time we called a play, Derek knew beforehand what plays would be coming, especially on defense. One thing me and my teammates all knew is when Derek was on the field there were two things that were certain. First, he was going to run hard and try and hit the other guy harder than he was going to get hit. Second is that Derek was always going to be in the right spot flying towards the ball. I think that's what made it the most fun to play with him, is just knowing that we had a guy on our team that was going 110 percent every play of the game from kickoff/kick return to running the ball on first down."

I was mentally and physically tough and never took a play off. No matter the challenge or adversity, I was able to reset, refocus, and move on to the next play. I was willing to mix it up and do whatever was asked of me because I loved to compete and do what was best for my team. I had great composure, and no situation was too big. I also had great balance, leverage, strength, power, and technique. Because I was so gifted, intense, and determined, I believe my teammates thought there wasn't anything I wasn't capable of on the football field.

"One of Derek's biggest advantages while on the field is that every time he had the ball it was all natural movements," one of my teammates remembers. "On kick return, it'd be a couple of smooth moves, and Derek would be down the sideline. On defense, it would be a one-read step, and Derek was in the hole, meeting the ball carrier. Or even on offense, he could switch into any role needed and perform really well. I think the microphone speakers were programmed with Derek's name and number; that's how good he was with or without the ball in his hands."

★ ★ ★ ★ ★

Before September 6, 2008, I believed I would have continued competing and succeeding at the highest levels in sports. "Any sport, he was good at," Michael Karel said. "Derek always wanted to be successful at the top level. I've been around a lot of athletes, and it's clear he would have easily gone on to college and competed at a high level."

Driving home from my last baseball tournament in Colorado just a few weeks before my injury, I talked to my parents about the tough decision I would soon have to make between baseball and football.

CHAPTER EIGHT

M y first season without baseball was in the summer of 2009. I was out of my routine and away from my team, which was devasting.

Before my injury, my days and seasons followed a prescribed pattern. I did the exact same things each week; or at least tried to. Mondays were laid-back because on the weekends, I would often be in an athletic tournament, and my team's final game would usually be mid-afternoon on Sunday. Tuesdays and Thursdays were typically spent in a gym or on a ball diamond because that was when I had practices.

Now, my days were a blur of hours at Madonna, doctor's appointments, and time at home. I had been somewhat okay with things while my brothers were in school all day, but it was hard once the summer hit, and they were running around to different sports practices and games. That was a new dose of reality as I realized that, from now on, my place would be in the bleachers, cheering others on. I was glad to be there for my brothers, but it was a gut punch.

My baseball teammates were lost without me, and I was just as lost without them. The memories we formed together in the previous summers created a brotherhood between us. Being stripped of that passion and love took a great toll on me, both physically and mentally.

I did have a few bright spots along the way that summer. While I was receiving inpatient care at Madonna, we met the Verzal family. Alexis Verzal had a traumatic brain injury after she was shaken at a daycare in Texas in April 2008. Like me, her prognosis wasn't great. Doctors told her parents, Brandon and Tiffany Verzal, that the most they could do was take their daughter home and hope for the best. Instead, they researched the best rehabilitation hospitals and chose Madonna. In the summer of 2009, Brandon and Tiffany included my story in their film *Pathways: From Brain Injury to Hope*.

And in late August, I returned to school. Three hundred and forty-three days after my injury, I walked into Malcolm Junior/Senior High to rejoin my class. I had reached another goal! I had a new routine, and it was grueling. I went to school in the mornings and back to Madonna each afternoon to continue rehab. I experienced some regression in the first month or two due to cognitive fatigue. I was exerting so much mental and physical energy at school that I had to back off on my therapy a bit.

I was working a lot on small motor skills, and it was exhausting. Little things like isolating my muscles and lifting just my index finger were extremely difficult, and I would get frustrated and mad. I was also concentrating on hand-eye coordination. With my background and expectations of myself, this was a very discouraging period. I would say things to my therapists like, "It's not working! I'm getting worse, not better!" They would try to slow me down, temper my expectations, and remind me that I was asking my brain to do a lot more work.

I did make straight A's my first semester back. It was reassuring to discover that I could still do academic work at my grade level.

In the fall of 2009, I was honored as one of the Madonna GOAL Award recipients. Now, when you walk into the new spacious, sun-lit entrance to the rehabilitation hospital, a video screen scrolls through stories of past GOAL award recipients. When my story appears on the screen, you'll read:

Derek Ruth of Malcolm, Nebraska, is a champion to those who know him, both on and off the football field or baseball diamond. While playing a youth football game on September 6, 2008, Derek suffered a traumatic brain injury. After two surgeries to save his life, he was transferred to Madonna's pediatric rehabilitation program. At first, Derek was so weak, just sitting in a wheelchair was a strain after short periods. With the help of his Madonna team and support from his family and friends, Derek made incredible progress. He used the bodyweight support treadmill to relearn proper gait positioning, going from struggling to stand with support to walking on his own. Derek achieved his first goal, leaving the inpatient program in time for Christmas. He returned in January 2009 for outpatient therapy in the Rehabilitation Day Program. To celebrate his achievements, friends organized "Team Derek" and participated in the Lincoln Marathon on May 3, 2009. Derek cheered on his supporters and crossed the finish line with his family—running the last few yards.

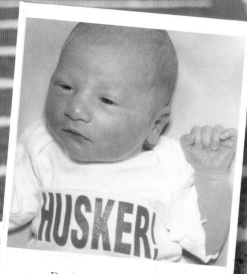

Derek Ruth, October 3, 1995

My baptism, October 22, 1995, with my parents and my sponsors, Uncle Jeff and Aunt Tracy

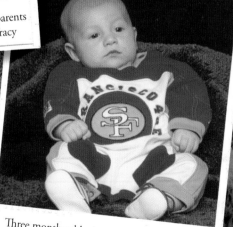

Three months old when Uncle Jeff was playing football for the San Francisco 49ers

Me at one year old

First day of preschool

Me at two—I always had a
football in my hands

Christmas Day, the year 2000,
in my new baseball gear

Nebraska football fan day with
my favorite player: Uncle Joel #45

2005 during my first baseball season
with the Lincoln Sox

2007: confirmation with my sponsor, Uncle Jeff, at North American Martyrs Catholic Church

7th grade football….
my final game, me returning a kick off

After Christmas mass on December 24, 2007.
My first Christmas with four younger brothers

#22 carrying the ball

My 7th grade school picture, taken one week before my injury

The final carry

September 6, 2008, the day of my injury in the ICU

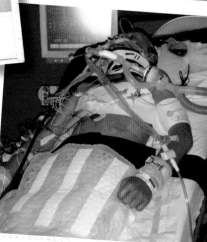

My first three days in the ICU—following my first surgery—elevated on a tilt table and being cooled

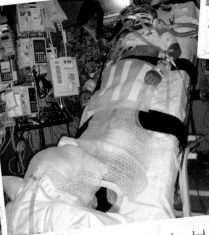

I would remain on a tilt table and cooled to minimize brain swelling for thirty-six hours

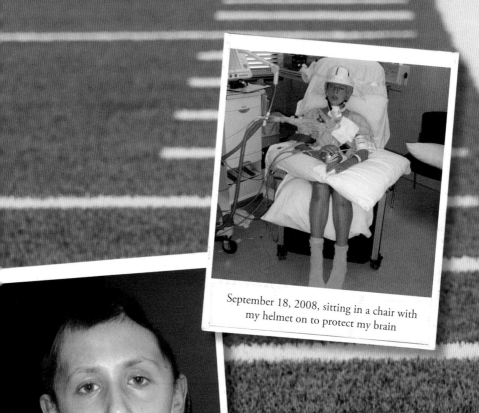

September 18, 2008, sitting in a chair with my helmet on to protect my brain

October 24, 2008, at Madonna Rehabilitation Hospital prior to my skull flaps being put back on. My head was concave on both sides

Shari Kopf and Joel Makovicka at the summit of Mount Kilimanjaro in Tanzania, raising awareness for traumatic brain injuries

July 19, 2012 at the Sanctuary of
Our Lady of Lourdes

My senior picture.
Graduate of the Class of 2014

Me, Corbin, Dad, Brenden, Mom,
Connor and Trevor

Me and my four brothers at my
Uncle's wedding

My mom and I during our trip to
the Holy Land

December 21, 2019, my graduation from the
University of Nebraska–Lincoln

My family

CHAPTER NINE

Once we knew I would survive, my family was determined to help me recover as much ability as possible and have the highest quality of life possible. My mom is a tenacious researcher. She spent hours and hours reading articles, researching medical treatments and trials, and contacting doctors. She left no stone unturned when it came to helping me achieve more.

While I was still an inpatient at Madonna, the physiatrist started working with my therapists on Botox injections. Botox kills the myelin on the sheath of the nerve, which means no signal is going to the muscle, so that it won't contract. It's basically a toxin, so you can only have so much Botox in your system at one time. My therapists would consult with Dr. Eric Hartman, and together, they would decide which muscles to inject. They calculated how much Botox I could have for my age and body weight. I would sometimes have between twenty and forty injections in one session. I had a lot of injections in my right arm. Between forty-eight and seventy-two hours after an injection, they could start working with a muscle to increase my range and reduce enough of the tone to stretch it out. The Botox would last three to six months, and then I'd have another injection.

I saw some good results, but my right hand was still very tight, so when Dr. Hartman went on sabbatical in the summer of 2009, Holly recommended we go to the Center for Pediatric Rehabilitation at Gillette Children's Specialty Healthcare in St. Paul, Minnesota, for more Botox treatments. Holly took the trip with us. She sat in the back with me, and I drove her crazy, changing music on my iPod.

"I think we listened to 10,000 songs on the way," Holly said. "You were like twenty seconds, new song; twenty seconds, new song. Can't we listen to one song for more than thirty seconds? After my boys became teenagers, I realized how normal that is."

A normal thing! I was doing something other thirteen-year-olds might do.

I've had several rounds of Botox over the years. I even had some injections in my mouth, but they didn't help much. I had treatments in Minneapolis, at the University of Nebraska Medical Center in Omaha, and back at Madonna with Dr. Adam Kafka. The first rounds of Botox injections were effective, but it got to the point where we had to weigh the benefits against how many toxins I wanted to put in my body.

People used to believe any improvement after a traumatic brain injury would happen within the first two years, but that's no longer the thinking, as many studies have shown the benefits of continuing treatment beyond two years. Doctors are discovering new treatments and innovative ways to rebuild neuropathways within the brain. Like the revolutionary cooling procedure that saved my life in the emergency room, I have benefited from some of those cutting-edge treatments.

In July 2009, I was featured in a *Parade Magazine* article by Lee Woodruff called "Can Brains be Saved?" The article talked about how advances in medical technology have helped me and other TBI patients like Lee's husband, Bob Woodruff. In January 2006, Bob was injured by a roadside bomb in Iraq while he was covering the war for ABC News. Lee Woodruff spoke at Madonna while I was there and met my mom. She remains a good family friend. Mom recalls Lee walking into my room, seeing me, and saying, "Wow." She understood what we were facing like only few people could.

One of the advancements that helped in my recovery process was hyperbaric oxygen therapy (HBOT). In mid-May 2010, only a few places in the country had hyperbaric oxygen chambers, and just a handful of those were using them for TBI patients. Dr. Paul Harch is an internationally renowned expert in using HBOT to treat more than 100 neurological conditions. The first TBI patient Dr. Harch treated was in 1989, a boxer 23 years after his last boxing bout, and from the year 2000 on, Dr. Harch decided to concentrate part of his practice on proving the effectiveness of HBOT in chronic TBI.

I came to his oxygen clinic at the exact same time Dr. Harch was conducting studies on veterans who had sustained a TBI. He felt I would be a good candidate for HBOT, which uses 100 percent pure oxygen in a pressurized chamber to help the body heal. None of this would be covered by insurance. HBOT is FDA-approved for treating burns, carbon monoxide poisoning, wounds, infections, and some other conditions, but not traumatic brain injury.

In the summer of 2010, after school had ended, Mom, Dad, and I headed to Dr. Harch's clinic in New Orleans to begin very aggressive HBOT. Before treatments began, I did a SPECT brain blood flow scan. This scan was abnormal and consistent with my injury.

I had forty treatments over four weeks. Each day, I did two treatments with four hours in between. I did that treatment regimen because that was the protocol Dr. Harch was using for the veteran TBI study at the time, and Dr. Harch was trying to make maximum use of my time. I had to shower with unscented soap and could not have deodorant or lotion or anything on my skin. Because of the high risk of fire when you're working with pure oxygen, I also had to wear 100 percent cotton clothing.

I would lie down on a hyperbaric gurney that was wheeled into the clear chamber—a specific gurney that is made for the hyperbaric chamber. After they closed the chamber door, I could see out, and the doctors and technicians could see in through the glass walls, but the only way to communicate was through an intercom. It took about five minutes for it to pressurize. In my case, I was at 1.5-1.75 times normal pressure; at this increased pressure, I was given pure oxygen.

During the first couple minutes of pressurization, it felt kind of like being on an airplane when your ears need to pop. Once the chamber was pressurized, the treatments were very relaxing. There was a television screen outside of the chamber I could watch, and the audio came through the intercom, but I generally slept during the sixty-minute sessions. With these conditions, your lungs can gather much more oxygen than would be possible by just breathing pure oxygen at normal air pressure. This extra pressure pushes more pure oxygen into your body. It also triggers the release of substances called growth factors and stem cells which help promote healing within the brain as well as the body.

I was exhausted between treatment sessions. My body was very tired, and I just really wanted to sleep. But after my second treatment of the day was complete, I would still work out and run on the baseball field near the clinic. I couldn't take time off from building muscle and improving mobility.

We started to notice results from the HBOT, and I felt an overall improvement in my quality of life. Before the treatments, I often had a dazed or foggy look, sometimes a blank stare with little expression. With the hyperbaric oxygen therapy, I was more engaged and alert. After 34 HBOTs, I had improved my leg strength, speed, coordination, walking ability, exercise, speech, hand strength, cognition, control of my laugh, and tone in my hands. I also had decreased right ankle pain and drooling. Functional activities were becoming easier; I was able to clasp my own seatbelt and get in and out of the shower by myself.

After 82 HBOTs, I experienced further improvement in all of these functions, but most noticeably, I was cognitively better, quicker, sharper with improved reading, comprehension, and short-term memory.

While we were in New Orleans, Mom and I stayed in a hotel. After two weeks, Grandma and Grandpa Makovicka flew down so Mom could fly home for a week to be with my brothers and Dad. At the end of four weeks, we went back to Nebraska, but we returned to New Orleans for another four-week session later that summer and some shorter sessions over Christmas and other school breaks the following year.

After the first forty-session round of HBOT, we consulted with a doctor who was doing innovative treatments with stem cells. My parents had studied and thought a lot about this. Because of our faith, we did not want to do any treatment that involved embryonic stem cells. We also did not want to travel outside the United States, where many people were going for stem cell procedures at the time. My parents had previously saved the umbilical cord blood from my two youngest siblings and even investigated using that.

We consulted with Dr. Gabriel Lasala in Covington, Louisiana, one of the few doctors who would take stem cells from one's own body, let them grow and multiply, and then reinsert them. We hoped the new stem cells would go into areas of my brain that were injured or had deficits and start regenerating some of that tissue. Again, my parents were willing to go to great lengths to help me regain my health.

We decided to explore Dr. Lasala's procedure. My stem cells were harvested from my L4/L5 lumbar spine, grown for approximately two weeks in a laboratory, and then reinserted into my spinal fluid when I returned back to Louisiana. They put me on a tilt table which would angle my head in a slightly upside-down position after the reinsertion to encourage the stem cells to go to my brain. The brain is complex, and it's often difficult to know what is going on inside. We did not notice any significant changes or improvements following the stem cell procedure.

My mom also had been researching glutathione injections. Glutathione is produced in the liver and plays a role in tissue building and repair. Mom was intrigued by the outcomes that Parkinson's patients were having with glutathione treatments. Some of my injuries were in the basal ganglia in my brain, which is the same area affected by Parkinson's disease. I also showed some of the same rigidity patterns that are seen in Parkinson's patients.

Mom contacted Dr. David Perlmutter in Naples, Florida, who did treatments with glutathione. Glutathione can be taken orally, but it is more beneficial if it is injected into the body, which allows it to cross the blood-brain barrier. We went to Florida, met with Dr. Perlmutter, and decided it would be a good treatment plan to try. In September 2011, I did a trial of daily glutathione injections. We made regular trips to Florida beginning that September and all the way to June 2012. In between visits, he gave us a prescription for glutathione to be injected at home in Nebraska. We made arrangements for injections two to three times a week. Dr. Perlmutter also had me on a regimen of vitamins and supplements to help my body. My muscles felt more relaxed, and I could verbalize a bit better with the glutathione. I experienced definite improvements in my overall quality of life and my abilities with the injections and treatments from Dr. Perlmutter.

My family has made many sacrifices throughout this journey to help me in any and every way possible. I'm so grateful for their continued willingness to do whatever it takes and to explore new therapies and possible treatments. They have provided such a great opportunity for me not only to recover but to continue to develop and heal. Without them and blessings from God, I really do not know where I would be, but it would be far different than where I am now.

CHAPTER
TEN

On September 6, 2010, two years to the day after I collapsed on the football field, my uncle, Joel Makovicka, began a climb of Mount Kilimanjaro in Tanzania. Five days later, he and his climbing partner, former Nebraska cheerleader Shari Kopf, reached the summit of the challenging 19,340-foot mountain. At the summit, they proudly flew the Nebraska flag for all families with children impacted by traumatic brain injuries.

Joel has always been one of my heroes. I was his first nephew, and some of my earliest memories are of watching him play football. When I was born in the fall of 1995, Joel and his older brother, my uncle Jeff, were playing for the University of Nebraska Cornhuskers. They won the national championship for the second year in a row. Jeff graduated after the 1996 season, but Joel was still on the team when they won a third national championship in 1997. Family lore recounts stories of my mom taking me to games when I was just a few weeks old, and in January of 1996, at just three months old, I took my first airplane trip to the Fiesta Bowl. The number-one-ranked Cornhuskers beat the second-ranked Florida Gators 62-24. Football is what our family does!

Joel and Jeff both joined the Huskers as walk-ons, which means they started playing college football without a scholarship. The Nebraska walk-on program is famous for giving athletes like my uncles, who came from a small high school where they played eight-man football, a chance to play for the Big Red. Both earned scholarships, and Joel became one of the most recognized fullbacks in Nebraska football history. He was named to the *Sports Illustrated* All-Walk-On Team in 1997 and was a captain for his senior season in 1998. Joel and I spent a lot of time together when I was growing up. I went to every single game he played at Nebraska, and after the Arizona Cardinals drafted Joel in the fourth round of the 1999 NFL draft, I traveled with my family to watch some of his professional games.

When I was playing youth football, my uncles would come to games when they could. "Derek was always one of those kids that was into athletics. He was a great athlete," Joel said. "I don't know this for sure, but having uncles that played at the University of Nebraska was one of the things that really got him motivated because he was around it since he was born. And that's something I think he took pride in."

Football is a family legacy. My dad played football at Kearney State College (now the University of Nebraska at Kearney). My Grandpa John also played football at Kearney. He led the nation in scoring in 1970 with 126 points and was named an All-American. All four of his sons played football at the University of Nebraska at Lincoln, and Joel played in the National Football League. The entire John and Connie Makovicka family was inducted into the Nebraska High School Hall of Fame in 2012. Grandpa John is also in the University of Nebraska at Kearney Hall of Fame.

I also hoped to play college ball one day, but my injury changed football, not just for me but for our family. After I was hurt, my dad kept my brothers out of football.

"I was scared for the boys," my dad said. "I was being very cautious, probably overly protective." After four years, when my brothers reached junior high, my parents decided to let them return to football. "It's just something that, for lack of better words, is in their blood. They love football. They have a passion," Dad said.

My uncles Justin and Jordan also stopped playing football for various reasons, my situation being one of them. They remained part of the Nebraska football team until after the spring game in 2009. At that point, Justin walked away from football, and Jordan transferred to Creighton University to play baseball.

★ ★ ★ ★ ★

After he retired from football, Joel became a physical therapist like his dad and sister. After my injury, he was there to help motivate me in rehab. When I got tired or discouraged, he pushed and inspired me. He helped me draw on the life skills I had learned through athletics.

"From a young age, Derek had goals and aspirations. And when you have that, you have this discipline to say, hey, this is what's laid out in front of me. This is what I have to do to get where I want to get. And I think that really helped him," Joel continued. "When you go through something like Derek's gone through, there could be good days and bad days, and it's human nature to want to give up on things. And, you know, he's probably gone through those days, but those are few and far between. I think he's been somebody that has always taken it in stride and understands that this is the work he has to put in to continue to get as good physically as he can."

Joel helped with some of my therapy at Madonna and later when I got home, but he wanted to do something more. He watched everything my family and I were dealing with and decided to climb Mount Kilimanjaro, the world's highest free-standing mountain, in my name. The goal was to generate awareness of families with children impacted by traumatic brain injuries and to raise funds to help alleviate the pressure those injuries place on finances and time.

"I thought about how determined he (Derek) is and figured I could make it up that climb," Joel told the *Lincoln Journal-Star* after his trek.

"You know, our family understands the things that a brain injury entails afterward, whether that's time in the hospital, the costs of that, the costs of therapy, the costs of maybe changing some things in the home," Joel said. "I wanted to do something."

So, Joel and Shari climbed. They did radio programs and used Facebook to help raise funds, then carried flags, jerseys, and other Husker memorabilia up Mt. Kilimanjaro to auction off when they returned.

"I tell people this, and I've told Derek that, you know, I played football at Nebraska and the NFL, and he's handled something like this better than anybody. And what he's been able to accomplish through all this, I think, is an inspiration. He's handled this way better than I could have ever handled it."

CHAPTER
ELEVEN

At the time of my collapse on the football field, the prevailing thought about traumatic brain injuries was that any gains a person makes would happen in the first two years. But that was starting to change. I was working toward my goal of returning to school with my class in the fall of 2009. I had endured three major surgeries and was still in a lot of pain. I was spending hours each day in outpatient therapy with the team at Madonna. Plus, I was doing additional physical therapy with my grandpa almost every night in the gym my family set up in our garage. I was exhausted, and though I was making great strides, some things weren't getting better. I couldn't speak, and I drooled constantly. My neck and my right hand were incredibly tight. I needed more specialized help.

That's when I met Ron Hruska and Lori Thomsen. One of the first things Lori did was give my mom a book, *The Brain That Changes Itself,* by Norman Doidge, MD. The book explores neuroplasticity—the idea that the brain can rewire itself, making continuing progress a possibility. I began a decade-long partnership with Ron and Lori that stretched not only my body but my mind—and I've progressed far beyond what many people ever thought possible.

Before my injury, I had never met Ron and Lori, but they knew my family. Ron grew up just a mile from where my grandpa lives, and Lori went to physical therapy school with my mom. Again, they are examples of God getting way out ahead and preparing the people I would need. Ron is the founder and director of the Postural Restoration Institute, and he and Lori take a different approach to physical therapy. They start with neurology, which, I learned, includes my tongue, lips, speech, chewing, and especially my teeth. I quickly discovered how much my bite impacted my balance and ability to move. They also taught me that some of my issues with tone and balance were caused by my brain not knowing how to inhibit the overuse of some of my muscles.

My first appointment with Ron and Lori was in April 2009. Some of our first goals were to help me regulate my swallowing and be able to speak. At that point, my mouth was open, and I couldn't close my lips completely. I was drooling a lot and constantly carried a towel with me. Whenever I needed to swallow, I had to use my hand to bring my jaw forward. This is the kind of stuff you don't realize can result from a traumatic brain injury.

I was a teenage athlete used to strenuous physical workouts that involved big muscle groups. Now, Lori and my mom were putting a handful of straws in my mouth to help with my lip closure or asking me to suck on pacifiers and bottles or blow bubbles. They even used a vibrator to help stimulate the feeling around my mouth. I rolled my eyes at them more than once.

"Derek's uncles, his grandfather, are really sports-minded people who played football," Ron said. "His dad was a star. His brothers are stars. They're athletes. They know orthopedics. So, imagine being in a family of all orthopedic-minded people, and Derek comes to this place. We're doing funny things with little pinwheels and straws and, you know, weird stuff. Can you imagine?"

Yeah, it was weird sometimes.

What happened to me in that football game was I lost my head. That's the way Ron described it. I lost my physical guidance system. I lost my balance. I lost my sense of placement. Where are my feet? Where are my front teeth? And how can I move my body forward if I can't find my teeth?

In a sense, Ron and Lori helped me find my teeth. Yeah, weird stuff.

Seriously, they taught me that I have two floors to think about: the one under my feet and the one in my mouth—my bite. I had to train my brain to assist my teeth and the neck muscles attached to my jaw. I was overworking my tongue and my neck to try to help stabilize my body. This caused incredible tension down the entire right side of my body. We worked a lot on centering activities so I could keep my neck neutral and also reach towards the floor with my arms. To help me stand up straighter, I did a lot of grounding work, which often meant changing something with my bite so I could better feel the floor under my feet.

In late April, Ron and Lori had me consult with a dentist, Dr. Michael Hoefs, who worked on expanding my palate and bringing my lower jaw forward. I wore a palate-expanding appliance for about eight months. Over the years, I have had many different appliances and treatments to help with my mouth closure. It took a team of amazing specialists, including Dr. Hoefs, Dr. George Adams, and Dr. Rebecca Hohl, to help me close my mouth.

"There was no book on Derek," Ron said. "Derek was an inspiration to us because he showed us things that I've never seen before, and you would not expect to see it in anybody else because the brain's unique only to you. And the way he injured his brain is unique. So, everything at that point was new. Everything was trial and error. Lori did things that you're not going to find in a book. We did things that would allow him to feel things in an unconventional way. And Derek works well with that because he's a young man. He has a lot of life expectancy. There is no limit."

When something wasn't working (and lots of things didn't), we had to work harder on other systems. In other words, we had to take what I could do and look for ways to complement that. It was an experiment, a discovery we were working on together. We were working around an incomplete system because of my tongue and teeth. Because I didn't have a good bite or a seal when I closed my mouth, I had a tough time with my feet and my vision.

I have always admired intelligent people, and Ron and Lori are some of the smartest people I have met. They taught me so much about neurology and how all this stuff works together. I learned about the three nervous systems: the central and peripheral nervous system, the autonomic nervous system, and the cranial nerves. Our cranial nerves run things like our eyesight, our hearing, and even our voice. My speech is a cranial nerve issue, while my arm and leg movement—my body flow—is governed by my central nervous system. The autonomic nervous system controls emotion. Ron said that, in my case, this third system is hyperactive because of limitations in the interplay between my cranial nerves and central nervous system.

"All these dentists and oral people were trying hard to get this central nervous system function back—muscles of the mouth, facial expression, gesturing, speech, lip closure, etc.," Ron said. "The cranial nerves are way deep in that brain stem, so that part of Derek's brain, his midbrain, was also damaged to some extent."

My injury had impacted my ability to regulate things processed with cranial nerves, like sight, speech, and facial expression. Now, my brain was trying to figure out ways to compensate for systems that were no longer working. That created a constant battle between the three systems, which led to increased extension tone (rigidness), anxiety, tremors, and clenching.

"These tremors are all part of a system called the midbrain, or his basal ganglia, and his thalamus," Ron explained. "Coordination for all this is right in the middle of his head, and he had a little bit of a bleed on top of that. He had some damage on the left side, so the middle of his head wasn't getting enough information from that side. He got too much information from one side, not enough from the other side. Simply put, he learned how to get as much as he could, but the timing and delay between the nervous systems makes it hard for him to regulate tension. Derek became somewhat 'disconnected.'

"His central nervous system was working well. But his cranial nerves—that would be the nerves that innervate and sense things, that are really taken for granted and are automatic—were not interplaying with both sides of the brain well enough. The hypoglossal nerve, a tongue nerve, is not completely injured but enough injured that the tongue management, speech management, vocal cord management impacted probably the most expressive function for Derek."

I appreciated learning about and beginning to understand what was going on in my body, what it had been through, and the challenges ahead. I would debate with Ron and Lori and sometimes ask both for their opinions about a new therapy. I was critical at times. I wanted to have all the information, and they were willing to answer my questions. We developed a deep mutual respect.

They also introduced me to one of their interns, Eric Oetter, a student physical therapist, and we bonded. Eric helped plant some of the same passion I had for weightlifting into some of the physical therapy work we did. He came to my house and worked out with me in my garage gym. Eric also understood neurology and helped integrate it with some of the orthopedic work I was already familiar with.

To help with my vision, we worked with prisms to trick my brain and help with my orientation. We worked with Dr. Heidi Wise. Different prisms would trick my body into relaxing, into feeling like I was steady and not about to fall. My brain responded! The tension—I can't describe how intense this tightness was—was rough, but the tension in my right arm immediately decreased with the prisms. And when that happened, I felt like my brain was actually working! It was a big deal, and I began to imagine what else my brain could learn to do. I talked with Ron and Lori about all kinds of ideas for other things we could try. Give me an inch of hope or a centimeter of progress, and I'll take it and run a mile. My competitive juices kick in.

And that also means I'm sometimes frustrated and impatient. Lori was constantly saying, "Slow down! Slow down!" My mind is always going a hundred miles an hour, and I wanted so badly for my body to keep up. And when I couldn't do something, I turned my frustration into fuel.

"I was glad that Derek had an attitude about something that either worked or didn't work because he was fighting," Ron said. "He doesn't give up."

I did have to learn to get out of my head. I relied on it too much physically. My head led my body around, which is a primitive reflex. I was using part of the old brain I kind of reset to when I was injured. When I wanted to walk forward, my head went forward first and a little to the side. Ron started calling me Derek 'Neck' Ruth.

"All head trauma patients have neck problems, and they're not orthopedic neck problems; they're neurological neck problems," Ron said. "Derek has a problem with his temporal mandibular joint (and that's all part of the neck) because of the accident. Temporal guidance is a challenge for Derek. For Derek to correctly, in his mind, move himself forward or side rotate, he has to overwork his neck to stabilize his cranium, so it stays between his shoulders when he moves."

Ron and Lori taught me about neutrality, and we worked on it intensely. I had to learn to keep my neck neutral. When my neck is neutral—in other words, positioned properly above my spine to cause the least amount of stress and pain—my arm movement is preserved. But if I lose the neutrality in my neck, my arm tightens up, and that starts a spiral. My arm gets tight, I get frustrated, then mad, and my anxiety increases. I must constantly work to keep my neck neutral.

Neutrality was made more difficult because I had left cranial torsion, which means my body twisted to the left, which can be a sign of trauma. We added Dr. Sarah Vander Pol to our team. She is an osteopath who worked with my cranium. We discovered a significant correlation between my neck and my cranium; my cranial torsion improved when my neck was in a neutral state. The cranial work with Dr. Vander Pol also helped me open and close my jaw more freely.

Living life after suffering a traumatic brain injury means that the further something is from my brain, the more difficult it is for me to sense and control it. My distal activity—my fingers and toes—can be tough. Utensil management. Buttons. Clothing. Eating. Recognizing where I am in relation to doorways and objects are all difficult. Lori used a Perplexus Ball, a ball with a maze inside. We tried playing a keyboard (which I hated), and I walked with a thick wooden dowel to try to get my hands to work together.

"Derek still made gains after two years," Lori said. "I want people to know there's hope."

I wasn't always sure about some of the things Ron and Lori wanted me to do, but I was always willing to try, even if I wanted to try it my own way. We disagreed and even argued at times, but in the end, what they did for me was some of the most important treatment I received.

CHAPTER
TWELVE

My family has been willing to go to the ends of the earth to get me the best treatment and opportunities, and that includes traveling to places known for healing, blessings, and miracles. From 2012 to 2019, I made pilgrimages to Rome, the Holy Land, and twice to Lourdes in southwestern France.

In July 2012, my family (minus Brenden, who was too young for the trip), my grandparents, and my Uncle Joel traveled to Rome and Lourdes with Father Raymond Jansen. Father Jansen was the priest at my grandparent's parish in Ulysses, Nebraska, and has baptized and married many of my extended family members. He often joined us for football games and family gatherings, and he and my grandfather would have coffee after mass every Christmas and Easter before Father headed home to Missouri. Father quickly became part of the Makovicka gang.

"Their family's like my family," Father Jansen said. "You know, kids running around, enjoying each other, getting together, and it's a lot of fun. And every time there's some big event—whether it's a tragedy or an uncertainty or a celebration—I usually get called right away and asked to pray.

I've prayed for football tryouts and stopped by the stadium to give somebody a blessing."

As my Grandpa John was driving to the hospital following my injury, he called Father, who immediately made the forty-five-minute drive to Lincoln. Father Jansen was one of the priests there to pray and provide counsel and support for my family in the aftermath.

When we started planning the trip to Lourdes and Rome, we invited Father to accompany us because he had studied in Rome, and he could lead mass for us in several locations. He knew the history, how to navigate the city, and where to find the best restaurants.

We approached the trip as a pilgrimage. Lourdes is known as a place of healing and miracles. In 1858, the Blessed Virgin Mary appeared eighteen times to Bernadette Soubirous, who later became St. Bernadette. Bernadette was fourteen years old when Mary visited her. I wanted to see the place where Mary visited a teenager like me. The appearances happened in a grotto outside the village. A church was built on the site, and water from a fountain in the grotto is collected in pools. People in need of healing go into the pools. The church above the pools is decorated with crutches, walkers, braces, and thank you's to Mary. People come from all over the world in every possible language you can imagine because it's a documented place of countless healings. We wanted to go there for that very reason; to see if it might please God that there be a miracle of healing for me.

We also decided to visit Rome so we could see the Pope and visit many of the beautiful basilicas and holy places. Our journey began with a half-day in Paris. When we arrived at Charles de Gaulle Airport, we saw NBA star Joakim Noah, a highlight for my brothers and me right off the bat. We made a mad dash around Paris and, in just a few hours, managed to see the Eiffel Tower and the Champs-Élysées, pray at Norte Dame, and grab a cab to a smaller airport to fly to Lyon.

We arrived in Lourdes that evening. It was such a peaceful, calming change of pace after Paris. Lourdes is a quiet and prayerful place. It's a serene French village, and every window is filled with a statue of Mary, a rosary, or Catholic goods. No motorinis blast past you, no big diesel-powered buses in front of you like we experienced in Rome. The people who come to Lourdes are not tourists but pilgrims seeking help from God.

That next day we had mass with some other visitors from the United States and then went to the baths. The baths opened at 9:00 a.m., but we were in line much earlier. Women and men go to different sides of the grotto. You get completely undressed and then are led to one of the baths to be submerged. I wasn't sure what to expect. The temperature of the baths is 12 degrees Celsius, which is equivalent to 53.6 degrees Fahrenheit. It was the coldest and purest water I had ever felt, let alone bathed in. But I was never cold or uncomfortable. An amazing sense of peace washed over me. As I emerged from the miraculous waters, I reflected on where I was and what had just happened. It was surreal to be standing at the Sanctuary in the exact location that Our Blessed Mother appeared so many years earlier.

While we were in Lourdes, we also walked the stations of the cross. Every Catholic church has fourteen stations that reflect the last day of our Lord's life. In Lourdes, the stations are outside with sculptures depicting each scene. Father had a special Brown Scapular blessing for me at station five, which shows Simon the Cyrene helping bear the Lord's cross. The Scapular blessing is for protection and a pledge of peace.

"Our Lord had a cross, and Derek has a cross," Father Jansen said. "And our Lord had someone help him carry that cross, and Derek has many people helping him carry his cross. In some way, Derek's injury and consequent physical difficulties are kind of a share in our Lord's passion themselves. So, I thought that station was appropriate."

We were drawn to the stations and returned to them several times.

That evening after dinner, I took a walk with my grandparents, and we came upon a torchlit procession and joined in. Pilgrims walked through the streets with candles, each reciting the rosary in their own language. I later learned that the procession began in 1863 and commemorates Mary's third appearance to Bernadette. Two people were with Bernadette that evening, and one carried a candle. It was an amazing thing to be a part of.

Our trip to Lourdes was brief. As we traveled the busy streets of Rome, we often remarked that we missed the serenity of that French village.

★ ★ ★ ★ ★

We flew from Lourdes to Rome and spent our first evening at a hotel near Roma Termini, which is a large railway station. The following day, we moved to a hotel closer to the center of town and visited St. Peter's Basilica.

"I always think that on a first visit to Rome, you go into St. Peters," Father Jansen said. "Catholics pray the Creed every Sunday at mass. And so, we knelt there by the bones of Saint Peter and recited the Catholic Creed."

The Vatican Necropolis, the ancient city of the dead, is buried under St. Peter's. Remnants of an entire city, its streets, and a cemetery were discovered under the basilica in the 1940s. We had signed up for a tour months before our trip, but we didn't realize there was an age restriction. Connor and Trevor were not old enough to go on the tour, which was disappointing because Connor loves history. Father Jansen had seen the ruins before, so he agreed to stay with Trevor and Connor. While we toured the depths of an ancient city, Father took Trevor and Connor to the cupola at the very top of St. Peter's. You must climb a very narrow, crowded staircase to get to the cupola. It's a very hot and congested climb. They failed to mention those facts to Grandma Connie, who is claustrophobic, before she and the rest of the family headed to the copula later. It was pretty traumatic for her, but she did make it to the top.

I didn't go to the cupola but instead went back into the basilica with Father. We visited *The Pietà*, Michelangelo's famous sculpture of Mary cradling the dead body of her son. Father had studied the statute when he lived in Rome. We talked a little bit about Michelangelo's thoughts as he created that sculpture. Michelangelo was criticized widely by some of the artistic community because Mary is portrayed as so young. His argument was that sin is what causes age. Father explained that it was Michelangelo's way of artistically witnessing the Immaculate Conception, which is a tie-in because in Lourdes, Mary revealed herself as "I am the Immaculate Conception." So, while my grandma was having a panic attack, we were enjoying a quiet time with *The Pietà*.

We also visited the Vatican Museum (another long line). The Sistine Chapel was part of the tour. We spent quite a bit of time in there, but it was crowded. You're in a line, and they just kind of push you through. Most of the beauty is on the ceiling, so you get tired of looking up and thinking about Michelangelo.

We returned to St. Peter's several days later to say mass. There are three other major basilicas in Rome: St. John Lateran, St. Mary Major, and then St. Paul Outside the Wall. We drove to all of those in our rental cars.

"It was a blessing of providence that we weren't arrested because you need special tags to drive in the oldest part of the city, and we just drove around absolutely carelessly without any regard for that at all," Father said. "I remember Joel was moved, especially by God hearing prayers, because we found a parking spot."

We were driving around looking for a parking spot near St. Mary Major, and Father said we should say a prayer. Joel was like, "What does God care about us finding a parking space?"

"Joel, God knows we're here to visit the church, so just say a prayer," Father responded.

He did, and all of a sudden, a car pulled out, and we snuck in. We wondered later why we hadn't asked for something better with that prayer.

Near St. John Lateran, we saw the Holy Stairs, which were the stairs our Lord ascended to stand before Pontius Pilate. St. Helena, the mother of Constantine, brought the stairs to Rome from Jerusalem in the fourth century. It is tradition for pilgrims to go up the twenty-eight steps on their knees. The marble stairs became so worn by tourists that wooden and glass steps were built over the top. You can peer through the glass on each step to see the marble underneath.

Stairs seemed to play a big role in our trip to Rome. We also climbed the Stairway to Heaven, 124 marble steps that lead to the church of Santa

Maria in Aracoeli. The stairs were commissioned as a gesture of thanks to the Virgin Mary. We climbed to the top with our backpacks and were sitting enjoying a lunch of food brought from our hotel. Father thought we needed a bottle of wine, so he headed back down the steps to find a bodega. Grandpa was worried that he was gone too long and made Joel run down the steps to find him.

All those steps and walking, especially on cobblestones, took a toll. It was painful. I had to stay back a few times. Eventually, I even got a new pair of shoes to help. We would visit sites and then return to our hotel in the late afternoon. At about eight o'clock we'd head to a nice restaurant that Father had picked, near one of the famous fountains. We threw coins into Trevi Fountain, and Trevor hit someone on the head. The person good-naturedly threw the coin back at Trevor. Trevor was our comic relief on the trip.

We spent a day taking a guided tour of the Colosseum and Forum. It rained, and my feet got soaked! We just marveled at the opulence that is still there. We also took a day trip to Pompeii. My mom and Uncle Joel love history and wanted to see every corner of the ruins and read every single plaque. The rest of us got tired of walking, so we sat down with our bread and cheese and had these refreshing drinks that came in huge lemons.

The highlight of our trip came on Sunday, July 22, when we went to Castel Gandolfo, the summer home of the pope. We drove sixteen miles from Rome to the beautiful setting on a hill overlooking an ancient volcano and a lake. The Vatican has an observatory there. We waited in line for hours before the gates opened. Security was very tight because the pope was there. A crowd of about 500 was yelling "We want Popa" in many different languages.

When Pope Benedict XVI (the sixteenth, for those who find Roman numerals confusing) finally came out, he blessed the crowd in several languages. His English was tough to understand, but Father Jansen interpreted and repeated everything the pope said. Seeing someone I hold such high esteem for in person was remarkable.

Even though Rome was chaotic, we found many places to pray—we were more than tourists; we were pilgrims. We were on a spiritual journey, a journey of personal growth to deepen our faith.

★ ★ ★ ★ ★

In October 2018, I took the trip of a lifetime to the Holy Land. My Uncle Joel planned the trip, and Father Jansen agreed to travel with us on one condition: We had to do extensive Bible study before we left so we would understand the context of what we would see and experience. So, we met at my grandma and grandpa's house each Sunday evening to learn about the sites in the Holy Land and read their references in sacred scripture. On this trip, it was just me, Mom, Grandpa John, Grandma Connie, Father Jansen, and my Uncle Joel, who came along with some of his friends and colleagues. Dad stayed home with my brothers.

We arrived the afternoon of Monday, October 16. The evening was falling by the time we were on the bus to our hotel. The guide tried to point out different areas and give us a sense of the Palestinian and Israeli borders, but it was hard to see much of anything in the dark. Our hotel was on the Sea of Galilee, so one of the first things we did the next day was take a boat tour of the sea. I also walked out into the sea with Father and Grandpa John. The Sea of Galilee is where Jesus walked on water and calmed the storm.

So many of Jesus' stories told in the gospels occurred near the Sea of Galilee. Capernaum, St. Peter's hometown, is located on the north shore. We went to the synagogue Peter would have attended and visited the Pilgrimage Church of St. Peter of Capernaum, a weird modern structure we thought looked like a flying saucer. You can walk right down to the place where Peter fished. We also visited a church built on the spot where our Lord appeared to the disciples after his resurrection.

It was snowing when we left the Midwest, but it was hot in the Holy Land. That first day, we had mass at the Church of the Beatitudes, where we got tucked into a stifling little crypt. The church sits on a hill overlooking the sea and is the site where Jesus spoke the Beatitudes in his Sermon on the Mount.

It was special for us to touch the sites that our Lord touched. One of my favorite places was the Basilica of the Annunciation in Nazareth. The church is built on the site where the angel came to Mary and announced the Incarnation. We had mass there and spent a lot of time in that little church.

We then took a bus to Caesarea Philippi. Again, Father made sure we understood where the name came from and what happened there. We read those passages of sacred scripture where our Lord takes his disciples up to Caesarea Philippi. When we arrived, everybody piled off the bus except us. Father would not let us go anywhere until we finished reading the passages. There is not much to see there unless you know what you're looking at. This was the place where our Lord said, "And I tell you, you are Peter, and on this rock I will build my church, and the powers of death shall not prevail against it." (Matthew 16:18).

We also visited Mount Carmel that day and later the Jordan River. (We packed the days full!) While it's popular for people to be baptized in the Jordan—where John baptized our Lord—Father made it clear none of us would be getting baptized that day.

"You can only get baptized one time," Father reminded us. "So, to pretend to do it another time is an insult to the Lord."

We all got in the river, but just to be clear, none of us was baptized in the Jordan.

We found it interesting that our rooms were always on the top floors of hotels. We soon learned that this is because of Shabbat, or the Sabbath. Jews are not allowed to do any work on Shabbat, not even push an elevator button, so the elevators automatically open on every floor. This makes a trip to the twentieth or twenty-fifth floor grueling. We discovered that taking the service elevators was much quicker.

Everything in the Holy Land was crowded, and you are not allowed much time to linger or pray, though I wanted to. In Bethlehem, Father and Uncle Joel ran a blocking scheme to allow me a few extra moments to pray and touch the ground where our Lord was born. After hours in the long line, Joel and Father were behind me and blocked the small entrance to give me just a few precious seconds.

I found peace in the places where our Lord and Holy Mother had been. The church of St. Anne is built on the birthplace of Mary. Next to the church, which is named for Mary's mother, is an extensive excavation of the Pools of Bethesda, where Jesus told a man who had been invalid for thirty-eight years to pick up his mat and go home. (John 5:2-9) For years, archaeologists or biblical scholars criticized this account in scripture because there were no pools there. But the pools were just buried. Now they are excavated, so we were able to go down the steps to the site. Father prayed for me there.

We celebrated a special event on sacred ground at the Mount of Olives. My grandma and grandpa were celebrating their anniversary, so my mom and uncle arranged access to the Garden of Olives, also known as Gethsemane. Father read their wedding vows and prayed a special blessing for them. We stood under ancient trees with gnarled trunks, and we were humbled to know we stood on the ground and under the trees where Jesus wept.

In Jerusalem, we walked the stations of the cross in the actual place our Lord walked. The Via Dolorosa winds through the streets of the city, with each station marked. We walked the stations super early one morning while it was still dark out. We had tried a few other times, but it was too crowded and chaotic.

We did have one unsettling moment in Jerusalem. We had wandered into an alley in the Palestinian District, where we were met with automatic weapons and cold stares. It was not necessarily unsafe, but definitely uncomfortable. It threw us for a bit.

Then we lost Grandpa John. We had walked through the cemetery in the Kidron Valley, where our Lord would have walked many times, and we saw the tomb of David's son Absalom. We also walked up a hill to the room where our Lord and his disciples had the Last Supper and then we went into King David's burial place. Our next stop was the site of the ancient temple, and that's where Grandpa John became separated from the group. The men had to enter one side of the ruins and the women on the other.

When we reached the security checkpoint, they wouldn't let us take our Bibles in with us. They said they would hold them for us, but Grandpa wanted to make sure we didn't lose those Bibles that had been with us the entire trip. So, he gathered them for the group to take back to our van. He waited for us where we had entered the temple but did not see us for a long time. He thought back to the encounter in the alley and Jerusalem and panicked. We had come out of an exit in a different location but finally found him. It was a place where we never felt comfortable. It's a flash point for controversy. The Muslims claim that it is the burial place of their prophet, but the Jews want to rebuild their temple. We were relieved when we left the temple site, all group members and Bibles accounted for.

While Grandpa was pacing and worrying about our safety, we saw the prophecy of Our Lord fulfilled. "As for these things which you see, the days will come when there shall not be left here one stone upon another that will not be thrown down." (Luke 21:6, RSV) We saw massive stones that had been thrown off the mountain when the Romans destroyed the temple and burned it. We had studied some of the history and learned the sad stories of torture and destruction.

We visited Masada on the eastern edge of the desert overlooking the Dead Sea. Herod the Great built two palaces there. Later, when Jerusalem fell in about the year 70, the few remaining Jews the Romans did not kill escaped and sought refuge in this mountaintop fortress.

We took a cable car to the top. From there, we could look down and see the siege equipment the Romans built. In our studies with Father Jansen, we learned how the Romans put Masada under siege by using Jewish prisoners to construct the ramparts. That meant the Jews sheltering in Masada had to kill their fellow Jews when they fought against the blockade. Masada had an intricate network of huge cisterns to catch rainwater, but the Romans below in the desert gave their soldiers just one cup of water a day as motivation for them to quickly defeat the Jews.

The ground around Masada is littered with missiles, which are huge stones the Romans would catapult all day long. Masada had little nooks where the Jews would let the children sleep to protect them from the missiles. Eventually, however, the Romans reached the fortress, and there were very few survivors. Some believe the Jews committed mass suicide rather than being killed by the Romans. Today, the Israel intelligence agency is called the Mossad, and members take vows of suicide before betrayal.

Later that day, we visited the Dead Sea. At first, the edge seemed like a dirty farm pond you'd find back in Nebraska. But we spent two hours frolicking in the water, covered in mud. It's so salty that you cannot get it close to your eyes. People in lifeguard chairs yelled, "Don't put your head in the water!" If you dive in, it's like a saltshaker in the eyes. And then you panic because the water is so buoyant that when you get on your back, you can't stand up. That was the weirdest thing, and we all had to try it—floating on our backs, not putting our heads under water. We couldn't splash, and we were floundering around like watermelons.

But the mud did feel nice. My mom and the other women in the group gave themselves facials and baked in the mud. Shops selling cosmetics made from the salty mud lined the shores. I'm not convinced it has worked any anti-aging miracles.

Our favorite thing on the entire trip was the Church of the Holy Sepulchre, which was our Lord's burial place and the site where he was crucified. Father joked that if we stayed there any longer, we would have to register as parishioners and take out offering envelopes. Early in the morning, when it was still dark, we'd walk through the streets of Jerusalem to the Sepulchre and then spend hours there praying. We had mass at the altar of Mary Magdalene. We spent hours in line there. We had our Bibles from our classes back in Butler County, and we would read about the events that took place on the ground where we were standing.

When you finally got to the site of the crucifixion, you could kneel and reach in to touch the ground where the cross of Jesus stood. It's not a large opening, and when I got up there, I somehow got my arm stuck.

"You're waiting in line forever, and people are shoving, and when you finally get to the place, they're like, hurry up, hurry up," my mom said. "They're giving you just a couple of seconds, and Derek went up there, he knelt, and he wasn't moving. We're thinking Derek was just praying."

My family was telling me I needed to move, but I couldn't. They finally came up beside me and saw that my arm was stuck. It was a very small space without much room to adjust my body and unpin my arm. My mom joked later that they would have had to shut down the monument and cut away the stone to free me. Fortunately, I was finally able to get myself unhitched.

After you view the site of the crucifixion (and get your arm back out in one piece), you stay in line to see the tomb. All of this is inside one big church. We loved this place. We felt drawn to it. People from all over the world were there. One day, we climbed the stairs on the side and sat watching people and praying. Later, we learned that you could spend the night in the Church of the Holy Sepulchre, but you needed to make reservations far in advance.

Each day, we prayed together morning and evening and had mass. Father had us download the iBreviary, an app on our phones that makes the Liturgy of the Hours available. The Liturgy of the Hours is the prayers that priests and the religious consecrated pray five times a day. The iBrievary contains almost all the Psalms, and you pray them each week. Sunday morning, our prayer began, "If I forget you, Jerusalem, let my right hand wither!" (Psalm 137:5). We were praying that as we arrived in Jerusalem. It was a beautiful thing.

Our trip home from Israel was an adventure. I got separated from my passport (my mom had it), and Father Jansen and I nearly got detained in Germany. After that was resolved, Father got very sick with a respiratory illness on the flight home. When we finally made it back to Nebraska, poor Father had to climb through a window to get into the rectory because his keys were in his luggage which didn't make it back until the following day.

CHAPTER
THIRTEEN

After Jesus appeared to me while I was in surgery in 2008, I remained very close to him and his mother. Once I became a little more alert at Madonna, I told my mom about my encounter with Jesus in Heaven. I don't remember exactly how I relayed the information, but she was the first person I told. She was not shocked because Mom knew the person I was and understood my prayer life and devotion to the most Holy Rosary.

When I came home for good from the rehabilitation hospital, some of my family members began asking about my experience. I remember sitting at the kitchen counter sometime in late January 2009 with my Uncle Jordan when he began asking me specific questions.

"Your brother Corbin told me that you were with Jesus in Heaven. Is that true?" he asked.

I told Jordan, "Yes, that is true." He just looked at me and did not say anything.

In early spring 2009, my cousin received her first holy communion on a Sunday. Afterward, we went to my uncle and aunt's house to celebrate. Uncle Jeff was my baptismal and confirmation sponsor. I told him about the appearance just as we were leaving. He did not express surprise but asked me several questions.

As the years went by, I kept quiet about my experience with Jesus in Heaven and only told a few select family members. Then, in the fall of 2012, I began attending Bible study at North American Martyrs. The class was called Seeking the Truth Catholic Bible Study, and at the time, we were studying the Synoptics in the gospels of Matthew, Mark, and Luke. Every Wednesday night, from 6:00 to 7:30, we had class. I was the youngest person in the class at the time. The rest were adults. We had weekly reading assignments, and in each class, we would split into three groups for the first forty minutes to go over what we'd read. After we were finished with the groups, everyone got together and watched a video lecture by Sharon Doran, the Bible study leader out of Omaha. One evening after class was over, I told one of my good friends that I had been with Jesus in Heaven. It was out of the blue, and my friend was a little shocked and overwhelmed.

After I told my friend about my experience, I was inspired to tell more people. So, I wrote a little two-paragraph paper telling people in my Bible study group what I experienced. I did not go into much detail; I just wrote that I had been in Heaven with Jesus and described my devotion to the most Holy Rosary. I did not explain what Jesus or Heaven looked like. I would guess there were ten to fifteen people in my group. When I shared my experience, several people cried, and those who didn't cry teared up.

As time went by in Seeking the Truth Catholic Bible Study, I became more comfortable and began telling everyone in the class about the appearance.

Five years after my injury, I had a second, tangible encounter with Jesus; two years later, I had a visitation from Mother Teresa, and the next year, more visitations from Jesus, Mary, and Mother Teresa.

Wednesday, July 10, 2013

I had been living in the aftermath of a traumatic brain injury for almost five years. I was still fighting muscle spasticity, especially in the right upper half of my body. My teeth did not touch anywhere so my neck was constantly working to keep my body stable, and I had a significant amount of tension throughout my face.

I was depressed. I was seventeen years old, and this was not the life I had imagined. I had tried everything humanly possible, from hyperbaric oxygen to glutathione to going to Lourdes and being submerged in the miraculous waters to being blessed by the Pope. Though I had experienced miracles, including surviving, being able to walk, and my brain functioning at a very high level, this was not what I wanted or expected. I spent countless hours reflecting on my life.

That Wednesday, I was having a particularly bad day. I had dinner with my family around 5:30 p.m. After dinner, my parents went to the Nebraska governor's mansion for an event hosted by my dad's company. My brothers were on the main level of our house, and I was with them. Shortly after six, I decided to go up to my room to pray and spend some time in silence.

The room was dim except for the digital clock on my nightstand. It was 6:20 p.m. I was talking to Jesus and Mary and began to weep because I was so unbelievably miserable and worn out. I just kept asking Jesus for help because I was scared at that point. I was afraid I did not know how to go on. Then, at 6:24 p.m., as I was saying a Hail Mary, Jesus appeared to me.

His presence filled the room. He appeared in front and slightly above me as I knelt next to my bed so I was gazing up at him. His robe was radiant white. His left hand pointed to his heart, and his right hand was raised to greet me. Two beams of light came from his heart, one red and one white. Jesus looked exactly like the image of divine mercy that Saint Faustina saw.

Jesus did not say anything but simply looked at me. His gaze restored a sense of hope and purpose in me.

I immediately texted my Uncle Jeff, told him what had just happened, and asked what I should do. Jeff was amazed and encouraged me to meditate on the appearance.

After that visit, I was inspired to pray the Divine Mercy Chaplet daily to revisit Jesus and be restored to that same sense of hope. As I mentioned earlier, I have had a devotion to the most Holy Rosary since I was confirmed at the age of eleven, but after this visitation, I added the Divine Mercy Chaplet to that.

January 6, 2015, and February 1, 2016

By the age of twelve, Anjezë Gonxhe Bojakhiu had determined to commit herself to a life of religious service. At eighteen, she left her home to join a religious order in Ireland. She never saw her family again. When she made her religious vows in 1931, she took the name Teresa. She began her work among the poorest of the poor in Calcutta in 1946 and would become known as Mother Teresa.

Father Jansen, the priest who traveled to Lourdes, Rome, and the Holy Land with my family and me, met Mother Teresa in the school year 1995/1996 at Mount Saint Mary's Seminary in Maryland. He told me about her life and inspired me to read and learn all I could about her. As a result, I began praying to Mother Teresa in June 2014, and I was helped through her intercession.

On January 6, 2015, I was in my bedroom sleeping, and at three in the morning, Mother Teresa appeared to me. She was directly in front and above me. Mother Teresa had on a plain white sari made of cotton with three blue stripes around the border and a veil on her head of similar design, just like the habits of the Missionaries of Charity. Her habit looked very clean. Mother Teresa stood with her hands at her side. She did not speak but only looked at me. Her eyes were open, but her mouth was closed, not so much in a smile, but still a comforting gaze. Mother Teresa's presence brought me great peace and caused me to reflect on my life.

After she appeared, I went back to bed because I was in utter amazement and shock. Later, when I woke up at around 7:30, I went into the kitchen and had breakfast. After breakfast, I laid on the couch near our kitchen and prayed the Rosary. I'm not sure if I told Mom or Dad first about the experience.

Mother Teresa appeared to me a second time on February 1, 2016, at 10:38 p.m. Again, she did not speak but brought me comfort and reassurance with her presence. I was awake but had my eyes closed when she appeared. Mother Teresa was directly above or a little behind my head.

I told Dad about the appearance the next morning, and all he said in reply was, "Awesome."

Both of my encounters with Mother Teresa occurred before she was canonized as a saint on September 4, 2016.

Thursday, March 24, and Friday, March 25, 2016

The Sacred Triduum has always been special to me. On Holy Thursday, 2016, my family and I went to the Mass of the Lord's Supper. That night, we commemorated the Last Supper our Lord Jesus celebrated with his disciples. That night marks the moment when our Savior instituted the Eucharist sacrifice of his body and blood.

Earlier that day, I prayed the most Holy Rosary and the Divine Mercy Chaplet. We went to our parish in Lincoln, North American Martyrs, for mass at seven that evening. My family and I received communion. Following the prayer after communion, everyone who was in attendance knelt as the priest incensed the blessed sacrament on the altar. The priest then carried the Eucharist (the body and blood of Jesus) throughout the church to the altar of repose, which at Martyrs was the cafeteria. The tradition is that Jesus goes into the garden of Gethsemane, and we believers follow and watch and pray with him that night. I spent an hour with Jesus in the cafeteria. During that hour, I had an overwhelming sense of His presence. Jesus appeared to me for a brief moment. I was unaware of the time or anything around me. I had my eyes closed when Jesus appeared. His body was perfect and without blemish. Peace washed over me.

As soon as I got in the car, I told my dad and my brother Trevor what had just happened.

The following day was Good Friday. I went to confession with Father Christopher Kubat at North American Martyrs. I had some religious articles I wanted Father to bless, so we did the confession face-to-face. After confession and the blessing, Father and I talked for a time before I went into the church, prayed my penance, and talked to Jesus. I prayed three decades of the Rosary.

I finished praying the Rosary at home and then joined my family at 3:00 p.m. back at the church to do the stations of the cross—the hour of Mercy when Jesus died on the Cross. I remained at the church to reflect and pray. Good Friday is a day of fasting in the Catholic faith, so my family and I just had a light dinner at home. After we were finished eating, my brothers went to see friends while Mom and I returned to North American Martyrs for the Celebration of the Lord's Passion. This celebration consists of three parts: the Liturgy of the Word, the Adoration of the Cross, and Holy Communion. The Gospel is an especially long one. We read the entire Passion Narrative from the Gospel of John.

While Father Kubat was reading the Gospel, I just kept asking Jesus to hear and grant the petitions I was asking for. Then, when we got to the part when Jesus said, "It is finished. And bowing his head, he handed over the spirit," I knelt and paused for a short time and said a little prayer, along with every other person at the liturgy. There is something beautiful about praying with a community of people. You feel a sense of connection. Once the Gospel reading was finished, Father Christopher Kubat gave a brief homily. Following Father's homily, we concluded the liturgy with solemn intercessions where we prayed for the salvation of the whole world.

We moved to the second part: the Adoration of the Cross. During this time, all gathered in a line took turns adoring the cross one by one, with a kiss, a bow, or some other gesture. I had to wait for some time before I was able to adore the cross. When it was finally my time, I grabbed the holy cross with my right hand, and I kissed the feet of Jesus. Again, I said a short prayer of only a couple of words.

Adoration of the Cross finally ended, and it was time for Holy Communion. I received Jesus in the sacrament of Holy Communion, and after I received communion, I was in my pew, just sitting there in a period of silence. Following the final prayer over the people, all departed in silence after genuflecting toward the Cross.

Mom and I got home at about nine that evening. I went up to my room to bed about 10:30 but could not sleep. A little after eleven, I got up, got on my knees, and prayed the Rosary for the second time that day. At 11:20 p.m. I was on the fifth decade of the Sorrowful Mysteries, which is the Crucifixion and Death of Our Lord, and the fifth Hail Mary when Jesus appeared to me.

Jesus was talking in his native language, Aramaic. As I was reaching out to touch the hand of Jesus the Holy Spirit came into direct contact with my body. My body then became unbelievably weak and flaccid, and I experienced an unbelievable amount of peace. I had no idea what was happening to me. I was weeping uncontrollably. This time, Jesus' body was beaten and bloody. Jesus' whole body was bleeding as if Jesus had just gone through His Passion. The Face of Christ Jesus was marked, bloody, and beaten.

I somehow knew the heart of Jesus was bursting with blood. Jesus' wrists were bleeding, and so were his feet. There was so much pain and anguish on his face, but it was also filled with great mercy. Words cannot even describe his heart. The head of Jesus was also bloody from the crown of thorns he wore. All the while, Jesus kept talking to me in Aramaic. I finished praying the Rosary at 11:24 p.m., and Jesus departed. I shook uncontrollably and continued to cry for a few minutes. When I finally calmed down, I put holy water on my head, then put my right hand to my head so the excess holy water would flow over it.

I waited until Easter Sunday dinner to tell my family about my Good Friday experience. Each of my uncles talked to me in detail about my encounter with Jesus. The conversations ranged from "You better be writing these things down" to "You know, only saints have these things happen to them."

Thursday, April 28, 2016

It had been a little more than a month since Jesus appeared to me twice during Holy Week, yet I still felt his lingering peace and nearness.

On the night of April 28, I got up to go to the bathroom. I went back to bed about 11:00 p.m. but could not fall back asleep. So, I knelt right beside my bed to pray. I told Jesus and Mary everything I had thought about that day and asked them for blessings. After talking to Jesus and Mary, I started praying Hail Marys. I felt relaxed as I prayed and dozed off a little, shutting my eyes. Then Jesus appeared to me, just as he had a month before and spoke to me in Aramaic. He did not talk to me for long, perhaps thirty seconds to a minute, and I honestly could not tell you how long the appearance lasted.

After Jesus appeared to me, I went over to my statue of the Blessed Virgin Mary and put my right hand on the Blessed Mother. Suddenly, I began to see images of a beautiful lady. I am not certain, but I believe I saw four images of the Blessed Virgin Mary. Mary did not say anything to me but the Blessed Mother brought me a great amount of peace and comfort.

In all four images, she was the prettiest person I have seen in my whole life! She had blue eyes and brown hair. Mary's blue eyes had tears in them. She wore a white veil on her head that went down past her arms. Mary had a light around her head that formed a beautiful crown. I am not sure if I saw the twelve stars around her head mentioned in the book of Revelation and often pictured with Mary because I was in awe. It was beyond awe. I saw her Immaculate Heart; it was awesome and bursting with light that words cannot describe. Mary's hands were out at her side in an open, welcoming gesture. Mary is very small in size and has very delicate features. I marveled at how the Blessed Mother's feet are very tiny, and her calf muscles are not defined. Her arms and hands were just as small and delicate but beautiful.

Though greater in size than the Blessed Mother, Jesus resembled her in many ways—his body, shoulders, hands, and feet shared many features.

My dad was the first person to know about these appearances. I told him a couple of days later after church in the car. He just looked at me.

★ ★ ★ ★ ★

That December was the first time I told a group of kids about my experiences. I had been asked by the North American Martyrs School to give a presentation to the sixth-, seventh-, and eighth-grade classes. At first, I was a little hesitant about letting a group of 200 to 250 kids know about what I personally encountered.

After I gave my presentation, many students had questions for me. I ended up having kids write questions to me because there was no way I could answer every single question that day. I have given the same presentation to sixth-grade classes over the years at North American Martyrs. The students are always very curious because not many people have experienced what I have.

CHAPTER FOURTEEN

After Mary appeared to me in April 2016, I had an overwhelming desire to return to Lourdes. I talked with my parents and grandparents about another trip, and my grandparents, John and Connie Makovicka, agreed to make the pilgrimage with me.

On Thursday, July 25, 2019, we left for France. We flew from Eppley Airfield in Omaha to Dallas-Fort Worth to get on a flight to Paris. The flight to Paris was nine hours and twenty minutes, taking into consideration the seven-hour time change. We flew through the night, so I mostly slept. We landed in Paris in the middle of the afternoon on Friday.

We had to take a cab to another airport to catch our flight to Lourdes. We saw many of the same incredible sites we had seen as we sped by on our dash through Paris in 2012. The Eiffel Tower was the most impressive, but my focus was on getting to the Sanctuary of Our Lady of Lourdes. Our flight landed late Friday night, and then we had about a forty-five-minute bus ride to our hotel, which was just a five-minute walk from the sanctuary. We went to bed immediately because we had a big day ahead.

We arrived at the baths a little after seven on Saturday morning. My heart was racing, and I was filled with a great amount of anxiety. Though I had been to the baths before, I did not know what to expect, let alone what to think this time. The urge to be here had been so strong since Mary had appeared to me three years before.

I was one of the first people in line at the baths. We waited on a bench for nearly two hours until the baths opened at nine. While we waited, I prayed the Divine Mercy Chaplet and the Memorare:

Remember, O most gracious Virgin Mary, that never was it known that anyone who fled to thy protection, implored thy help, or sought thy intercession was left unaided. Inspired by this confidence, I fly unto thee, O Virgin of virgins, my Mother. To thee do I come, before thee I stand, sinful and sorrowful. O Mother of the Word Incarnate, despise not my petitions, but in thy mercy hear and answer me. Amen.

I also kept repeating in my head, "Jesus, I trust in you!"

About 8:10 a.m., or just a little later, the people in line for the baths prayed the most Holy Rosary to Mary. The Rosary concluded around 8:40 a.m., and then the doors to the Lourdes baths were opened. The feeling that washed over me was something I had never felt before in my life. There are multiple baths, some for women and some for men. My grandfather and I were one of the six people in the first group to be taken to be submerged in the miraculous Lourdes water.

We removed our clothing and wrapped towels around our waists to cover our genitals. They took us to the baths one by one to be fully submerged. I was third. My heart was beating at an unbelievably high rate, and I just kept making the sign of the cross and praying Hail Marys over and over in my head because I was very, very anxious. When it was finally time for me to go behind the curtain, two people, one on each side, accompanied me. That way, I could interlock arms with them so they could help me get into the baths.

I stepped down into the miraculous water, and then the two gentlemen who had interlocked my arms with theirs tipped me back, and my whole body up to my head was completely submerged in the water. As I described during my first experience at Lourdes, the water is 12 degrees Celsius, equivalent to 53.6 degrees Fahrenheit. It felt cold and pure. However, as the two gentlemen brought me up out of the Lourdes water, I did not feel cold or even wet. It was a weird sensation.

We dressed and met my grandmother just outside the baths. We spent some time praying before we went to breakfast. Over breakfast, we studied a map of the entire grotto and planned what we would do. We agreed on a meeting place right in front of the Basilica of The Immaculate Conception, and I spent the day exploring the entire grotto and identifying the things I would do regularly while we were there.

When Our Blessed Mother appeared to Bernadette in 1858, she instructed the young girl, "Go and drink from the spring and wash yourself there." Bernadette then discovered a spring that no one knew existed until that day. That spring feeds the baths where pilgrims bathe and runs through taps throughout the sanctuary. While the lines at the baths are always long, there were no lines at the eighteen Lourdes' water taps. The number eighteen symbolizes the number of times Our Blessed Mother appeared to Bernadette. I visited the taps several times a day. I put my hands and entire arms under the taps so the miraculous waters kept flowing over my arms and hands. Then I put my head under the taps and let the waters flow down my entire head. My hair was damp almost the entire time we were in Lourdes. Finally, after letting the waters flow down every visible area of my body, I put my mouth under the taps, drank the water, and let it run over my tongue.

We went to mass at the Basilica of the Immaculate Conception on Saturday evening to fulfill the Sunday obligation. Mass concluded, and we had dinner just outside the entrance of the grotto. We had a good and fulfilling meal that evening because we had not eaten anything since breakfast. Once we were finished, we prayed the third day of the Novena to Our Lady of Knots in our hotel room. This is a special devotion to Mary, who helps undo the knots in our lives. My grandparents and I began the Novena

Thursday while we were in the Dallas Fort Worth Airport. Later that night, we went back inside the grotto to walk around and plan what we would do Sunday. Just as the sun was setting, I returned to the water taps to let the Lourdes water run across my body and to fill a bottle to take back to the room so I could bless myself before I went to bed.

We were back in line for the baths at 7:00 a.m. on Sunday. Again, Grandpa and I were some of the first in line. A little before 7:30, I told Grandpa I was going to the bathroom. Instead, I made a quick stop at the water taps to let the miraculous waters run down my right arm and hand, drink a little, and finally put my head under. When I returned to the line about five minutes later, Grandpa looked at me, noticed my wet hair, and knew exactly where I had been.

When the Rosary concluded at around 8:40 a.m., we were taken back into the rooms to disrobe. Two gentlemen interlocked arms with me when my time came to be submerged. I was submerged full body. Then, rather than exiting the Lourdes baths, I leaned back and was submerged again in the waters. So, I got submerged twice that day!

We spent the morning at the grotto, visiting the exact spot where The Virgin Mary appeared to Saint Bernadette. We just sat there for a moment and prayed the Novena before we went to mass at the Basilica of The Immaculate Conception. That afternoon, we visited every church located in the grotto. It took the rest of the day.

We followed the same morning routine on Monday. After we were submerged in the baths, we walked the stations of the cross. It took a couple of hours to get through the Way of the Cross. After we were finished, we returned to our hotel room for a little rest. Once we were finished resting, we ate dinner and went back inside the sanctuary.

Between two and three o'clock in the morning on Tuesday, my cellphone began to vibrate with text messages continuously. It was 7:30 Monday evening back in Nebraska, and my home parish, North American Martyrs, was holding a prayer service for me. Father Brian Connor, the priest at North American Martyrs Parish at the time, put the consecrated host, the

Body of Jesus Christ, on the altar in the monstrance. While the Body of Jesus was on the altar, Father Connor had the parish family pray the Rosary and the divine mercy chaplet for the intentions I had. The people continued to pray, asking Jesus to grant those intentions. The prayer service ended at eight Monday night in Nebraska, 3:00 a.m. in Lourdes.

Tuesday was a peaceful, relaxing day for me. I felt loved and supported by texts and prayers from home. After we finished bathing, we walked through the sanctuary. That evening, I spent a good hour at the Lourdes water taps, letting the waters run on every area of my body that was not covered by clothing.

Wednesday was the final full day at the sanctuary. After our morning ritual at the baths, we toured the town of Lourdes on a trolley. That night, we went to the Marian Procession. The Procession began at nine, just after the sun went down. Let me tell you that the Marian Procession was one of the most incredible things I have ever witnessed. The Procession began, and then the Rosary began just minutes later. Each pilgrim carried a candle, and it was absolutely amazing to hear the Rosary being recited simultaneously in many languages—people from all over the world praying the exact same prayer. The leaders of the Rosary were standing just below the Rosary Basilica. Every two Hail Marys, the leader of the Rosary would change, as would the language. I could not identify all the languages spoken, but I knew English was one. While the rosary was being prayed, "Ave Maria" was sung after the conclusion of each decade of the Rosary. Through all of this, the Marian Statue kept proceeding throughout the sanctuary. The Marian Statue was just below the Rosary Basilica when the Rosary was completed. The Procession lasted for a little more than an hour.

Now, it was time to head home and prepare for my final semester of college.

CHAPTER
FIFTEEN

*"Not the victory but the action; Not the goal but the game; In the
deed the glory."*

—Inscription on the University of
Nebraska–Lincoln Memorial Stadium

On Saturday, May 10, 2014, I walked across the stage and received my
diploma from Malcolm Public Schools. I had achieved my goal of
graduating with my class.

High school had been brutal, and I was ready to leave that chapter of
my life behind. My time in high school seemed to move on like a sinner's
prayer—long and drawn out. I did not get to experience many of the things
my classmates did, such as driving to school, playing sports—the list goes
on and on. To be honest, I had some good friends leave my side as our lives
went in different directions. It was time for something new.

It had always been my goal to attend college and that hadn't changed.
Before my injury, I thought I would follow in the footsteps of my mom
and dad, my uncles, and my grandfather and attend college on an athletic
scholarship. Unfortunately, recruiting trips were another one of those experiences I would never have.

The University of Nebraska–Lincoln was founded in 1869 and original-
ly occupied four blocks at the northern and western reaches of Lincoln. By

1909, nearly four thousand students were enrolled. Memorial Stadium was built in 1923 with a capacity of 31,080 and soon dominated the campus landscape. While the university has many strong academic programs and is the leader in all kinds of research, to me Memorial Stadium epitomizes Nebraska and the Nebraska way. The phrase "Nebraska Way" has come to mean a lot of things over the years. To me it means striving for excellence by putting everything you have and giving maximum effort all the time. By the time I was preparing for college in 2014, more than 25,000 students attended UNL, and the stadium could accommodate 87,147 fans. As we are fond of saying, on game days, Memorial Stadium is the third largest city in our state.

So, I set my sights on the University of Nebraska–Lincoln, but one thing stood in my way: I had not taken a foreign language class in high school. Because I still had a speech impediment, learning to verbalize in a foreign language was out of the question. That's when two friends helped make my appeal to the university for admission.

Even though I was no longer competing on the field, the connections I made through youth sports proved valuable. I met Tim Clare in 2006 when I played in the same baseball organization as his son. Tim was elected to the University of Nebraska Board of Regents in 2008.

I first met UNL football coach Bo Pelini in the fall of 2008. At that time, my uncles Justin and Jordan were playing for Coach Pelini and the Huskers. When my ordeal took place in September, Bo made several trips to the trauma center to see me. He spent time with my family while I was in the ICU. But I really got to know Bo in the spring of 2013. The first time I remember talking to him was during a baseball tournament. My brother, Corbin, and Bo's son, Patrick, played on the same select baseball team. Sometime during that tournament, Bo and I started talking. We connected over our shared faith and competitiveness.

"That was the first time I had ever spent any time at length with Derek, sitting there talking to him," Bo said. "And he made a huge impression on me, I'll put it this way. You know, if you go through things like he did, you would think that your faith can get shaken and with him, it's only made him stronger, and that's a testament to who he is as a man and to his character."

After that day, Bo and I had several conversations at baseball games. When the season was over, the Pelini family hosted a party at their home where we talked about several things, including my trip to Rome the previous summer.

"I haven't been there yet, but I'm going," Bo said. "That's probably one of the only places in Europe I'd really like to go and that's kind of on my bucket list and it's really because of the conversation I had with Derek. He told me about the history and the things that they experienced when they were in Rome and his faith in God oozed out of him. That conversation we had is something I think about a lot."

Toward the end of that evening, Bo asked if I planned to attend the university. At that point, I wasn't sure it was possible, but Bo said he'd help make it happen, and he did.

Tim and Bo both wrote letters on my behalf, asking the university to admit me.

"That was a no-brainer," Bo said, recalling that letter of recommendation. "I'll put it this way; it was one of the easiest letters I've ever written. With Derek, it was just say who he is. I know one thing: Everybody that came in contact with him during his time at University of Nebraska is a better person for having gotten to know Derek ... the university's better for him having gone there."

But Coach Pelini went beyond writing letters.

"When Derek was ready to go to college, I knew they were going to have some challenges as far as just the logistics of it, all the things that he was going to be going through, the newness of it," he said. "And I said whatever I could do to help the family and help Derek to make it a good experience for him, I was all for it."

I was accepted into the university and started classes there in the fall of 2014. Bo and my parents came up with a plan to handle the logistics of navigating campus. My parents would drop me off at the stadium and I would hang out in Bo's office until time for class. I walked to classes with some of the football players. When classes were over for the day, I would go to the academic study center in the stadium and do homework.

Everything worked smoothly until I wandered off on my own one day to explore the campus. The players I usually walked to class with didn't know where I was. They contacted Bo, who called my dad. There were a few minutes of panic until someone saw me. I didn't realize I had caused such a stir.

"I remember his first week at Nebraska, Derek was in and out of the office a lot, especially that first week while he was kind of getting the lay of the land," Bo said. "And it was just fun to watch him get more and more comfortable every day and grow into that portion of his life. And you know, he always had a smile on his face. And that, to me, is special. It was fun. It was just so much fun to be around."

Bo introduced me to Dennis Leblanc, now Nebraska's Executive Associate Athletic Director for Academics. Dennis helped me decide which classes to take, recommended professors, and set a timeframe for graduation. Coach Pelini opened many doors at college for me, and I took full advantage of every opportunity I received.

Coach Pelini also welcomed me to be around the football team as much as I wanted. I was able to hang out with the players and coaches, and on game days, I sat in one of the coaches' boxes.

"I think it had to have been hard for Derek; it had to be a process to be around football again after everything he's been through," Coach Pelini said. "Being around us, I think he became more comfortable with it. I know that growing up, he had a love for the game, and I'm sure that he went through a time where he probably didn't want to be around it. That time he spent with us, maybe brought it back into the fold for him and kind of rekindled his love for the sport."

Coach also gave me the gift of putting the game in perspective.

"No matter what, football—for me, for him, for everybody—football ends. And unfortunately for Derek that happened a little sooner than he would have liked. But like I said, what he's overcome and what he's learned through it, he's become an example for people.

"A lot of people would wilt under the adversity that he faces. Derek has gotten to the point in his life—I don't know if it was like that right off the bat—but now, he embraces it, and he's fought back through the help of his family, his loved ones, and the people around him. It's special what he's been able to achieve. Most people facing the things that he has faced would not be in the position he's in right now. He's one of the strongest people I've ever been around."

Like many young people, college gave me new friends and a new perspective on life. I liked the freedom and atmosphere of college. On Saturday, December 21, 2019, I graduated from the University of Nebraska–Lincoln with a degree in sociology. When I walked up to the stage, my good friend Tim Clare handed me my diploma. I'm so grateful to Tim, Dennis Leblanc, and Bo Pelini for what they did to help make that moment possible.

CHAPTER
SIXTEEN

Though I have endured unspeakable heartache, I have learned the greatest strength lies in resilience. I have come to understand that to propel our lives forward and reap the rewards, we must take risks, break our boundaries, and be brave enough to go against the odds.

My parents taught me that when tragedy strikes, the only way forward is to keep going, to keep moving, and to find solace in the next task at hand. There is no time for lying in bed wallowing and giving up. Life is a competition, and it is not fair, but it is an opportunity to conquer the unconquerable.

From the morning after my injury until this morning, my mom has gotten up each day and moved forward. My mom's friends commented that during those months she was sleeping on a couch in my room at Madonna, she'd always be up early and have her makeup on and hair done, ready for the day.

My dad has often told me, "As you go through life, a lot of times you think you're busy or overwhelmed, but when your back is against the wall, it's amazing what you can get done and how you can do it if you absolutely have to."

My brother Corbin was ten when I was injured. As the oldest sibling, he remembers the most about me before my injury. I recently asked his perspective on my life.

"Derek was obviously a great athlete, number one," Corbin said. "From a young age, he was a leader, and after his injury, he was almost more inspiring. Most people, if this ever happened to them, they would not be religious or they would say, why would God do this to somebody? But it brought him closer to God. He graduated from high school and from a Big Ten university. He is a motivated person. He wants to touch people. He motivates me."

For most of the first thirteen years of my life, I strived for excellence, pushing myself to the limits and never allowing myself to stay stagnant. My drive and enthusiasm have remained undying despite everything I have been through. Yes, some of my childhood dreams have gone up in flames and vanished, but that's not why I'm sharing my story.

Despite all I have lost, I am determined to cherish the good moments. I survived the toughest test of all, and from it, I resolved never to give up, to keep striving forward and living life with passion and ambition, never shying away from the impossible. Dreams must be taken seriously, and with courage from prayer, we can accomplish anything, even against the tide of time.

It has been a challenging journey, but I hold on to the following truths: Faith and family come ahead of all else. My parents taught me the importance of my Catholic faith and to value family, displaying this in their own lives. I am blessed to have such an amazing support system in my parents and grandparents. I'm beyond grateful for the older generations that led by example, showing me how to love God faithfully and love those around me.

I don't exactly agree with the popular sayings that God never gives you more than you can handle or that his hardest battles are reserved for his toughest soldiers. I think you should cherish every moment of good luck, persevere through every struggle as if it were a game of survival, and trust God.

Chapter Sixteen

Life is like a game with an unknown outcome—it takes courage, ambition, and resilience to keep playing. Don't be afraid to take risks; you will be rewarded for your courage and hard work.

I know that God is faithful.

Even when the shadows of life surrounded me, and all seemed lost, I knew he was there. He has answered my prayers and has been present with me. I have cried out to God over and over and over, and I will continue to cry out to Him. God has offered me his loving embrace through the appearances of His Son, the Holy Mother, and Mother Teresa, gifting me with tangible reminders that He is present in my life. Miracles have come through the help of doctors, nurses, therapists, family, friends, and the thousands who have prayed for me along the way. I am ever so thankful for their kindness and support as they have helped me spread the light and share God's glory.

During my time in heaven, Jesus gave me a choice, but I had no idea what that choice would entail. I believed I would come back to Earth and continue living like I had been for the first twelve years of my life. I had no idea the trials and tribulations I would face in order to regain my life, and it has not been easy, but I would make the same choice—I would choose this life.

ACKNOWLEDGEMENTS

Writing a book is harder than I thought and more rewarding than I ever imagined. I am extremely grateful to Cindy Conger for her editorial help and guidance in writing my first book. Without her nurturing, this endeavor would not have been possible.

To my family and friends who stood by me, I express my deepest gratitude for their unwavering support throughout this journey.

To Father Raymond Jansen for his guidance and friendship.

I want to thank the priests at North American Martyrs Catholic Church and throughout the diocese of Lincoln, Nebraska, and the members of North American Martyrs Catholic Church for your continuous prayers, love, and support.

To Father Sean Kilcawley for your daily visits to Bryan LGH West and Madonna Rehabilitation Hospital during my inpatient stay and your continued support throughout my rehabilitation process.

To the doctors, nurses, and staff at Bryan LGH for their quick response and innovative techniques in my initial care.

I would like to thank the entire Madonna Rehabilitation Hospital team for their care during my rehabilitation.

To Bo Pelini, Dennis LeBlanc, and Tim Clare for their help throughout my college career at the University of Nebraska–Lincoln, from help with admittance to class schedules and the daily ins and outs of college. They made my goal of a college education a reality.

To Michael Karel for his unending support.

To Lee Woodruff for her writing inspiration, leadership, and contribution to my book.

A sincere thank you to all the generous people who agreed to read this book and write endorsements on my behalf, and finally to all those who have been a part of my life.